Culture

KEY CONCEPTS

Published

Culture

Fred Inglis

polity

First published in 2004 by Polity Press Ltd.

Polity Press
65 Bridge Street
Cambridge CB2 1UR, UK

Polity Press
350 Main Street
Malden, MA 02148, USA

ISBN: 0-7456 2380-8
ISBN: 0-7456 2381-6 (pb)

A catalogue record for this book is available from the British
Library

Typeset in 10$\frac{1}{2}$ on 12 pt Sabon
by SNP Best-set Typesetter Ltd., Hong Kong
Printed and bound in Great Britain by MPG Books, Bodmin,
Cornwall

For further information on Polity, visit our website:
www.polity.co.uk

Contents

**For Sasha and Harriet,
keepers of the culture**

Foreword

An introduction to a book is much like an introduction to a person, and similarly, perhaps, not much listened to. None the less, it is worth announcing here that this book is *not* intended as a short directory to all that has most recently been written on the topic of culture. There are plenty such books around and, I confess, the contemporary habit in academic writing of assembling more or less trite summaries of other people's work, and disfiguring the prose at the end of every second sentence with a scattering of references, seems to me calculated to turn thought to lead and the eager reader into concrete.

What, on the contrary, I have attempted here is threefold: it is, first of all, a conceptual history written according to the precepts of what is sometimes called 'Cambridge historicism', following the precepts of that school's great originator, Quentin Skinner, whom I am proud to call friend. Secondly, the book prefigures an *argument* as to the necessity, vacuity and usability of our key concept in intellectual and everyday life. Finally, I have also much sought to *move* the reader with a sense of his and her duties to culture; to call each to the militant colours of the cultures to which we owe our very selves and our keen sense that life is so very worth living.

Most of this book was written and then, following the strictures of Polity's acute and admirable readers, rewritten while I was Fellow-in-Residence at the Humanities Institute,

University of Connecticut, during the academic year 2002–3. I am pleased to be able to thank in print its director Dick Brown, first and prompt reader of my first draft of *Culture*, its secretary, JoAnn Waide, and my fellow Fellow, Chris Clark, for their benevolence, hospitality and large tolerance towards my assorted requests for help. Quentin Skinner, already acknowledged, is a powerful presence in the whole thing. Krishan Kumar, now of the University of Virginia, gave me freely, as usual, of his ideas on the matter during my visit there, as did Graham Murdock in the nick of time, and Richard Howells whenever I appealed for help. Paul Terry and Susan Hodgett were early readers of the manuscript, and careful and kindly in their commentaries. My two dedicatees have, therefore, a lot to answer to, and two lifetimes in which to do so.

1
Birth of a Concept

I

It nowadays seems impossible to describe the most commonplace details of everyday life without using the word
'culture'. A report by government inspectors upon a school
may refer to 'a culture of failure', upon a prison to 'a culture
of secrecy'; sociologists, newspaper commentators, and moral
critics may all happily refer to the 'consumer culture' within
which we all of us equally live and move and have our being;
anthropologists have for a century or more referred to the
peoples they study as not just having but being 'other cultures' – for some writers 'primitive', even 'savage' (though
not necessarily with a pejorative inflexion), frequently self-
sufficient or autonomous. This way of using the word has,
under the pressures of a globe more and more conscious of
its own globalization, found its way into the everyday conversation of, inevitably, the culture.

Indeed, the idea of the conversation of culture as being
what constitutes the very concept itself is one to which we
shall later return at some length. Perhaps one of the deepest,
certainly one of the most absorbing, puzzles in human
enquiry is found in the mobile relations between our picture
of social reality and the words (let alone the concepts) which
assemble it for us.

I say 'assemble'; the more usual word is 'construct', not least because of a powerful book of 1967 famously entitled *The Social Construction of Reality*,[1] which became, quite rightly, one of the sacred texts of a school of social thought and a mode of analysis. This we might style the school of social constructionists, and by that would mean those who believed, and who practised their enquiries in the belief, that our real world is made up (constructed) by the collaborative efforts of a strictly human society. Thus, what we think of as the world-out-there is directly a product of complex interaction between the world-out-there and our language. Reality materializes at the moment when actuality meets the concepts and the self-understanding of human beings endeavouring to bring that world more or less under human control.

The argument was so taken to heart, both in and out of academic thought, that it became compulsory to enclose 'reality' within inverted commas in order to emphasize its constructed, even invented status as an object of enquiry. From this followed a view of the consequent impossibility of ever saying anything solid and endurable about a real world which could not be looked at and comprehended without the powers of human recognition. This attitude, it must be added, has become so exasperatingly pietistic that John Searle[2] wrote a revision of the argument showing how exactly true it is to say that the world-as-we-understand-it is unavoidably the product of exchanges between eyes, brains, facts, things, and words, but that the fact of those exchanges is absolutely no reason for putting reality in inverted commas. The thing we make up out of our perceptions and concepts as applied to objects and their properties is no less real because we have made it all up.

These clashes have coincided with the rise to universal prominence of the word 'culture', and whatever it is in human conduct which the word refers to. For when people say that a bankrupt corporation lived in 'a culture of suspicion', or that the business world itself is characterized by a 'culture of aggression', or even – as one celebrated anthropologist did of the groups he was studying – that a clutch of Hispanic American families occupied 'a culture of poverty', they are trying to catch hold of something as naturally human, as pressure-heavy but as invisible as air, which is at the same time wholly an artifice, a human artificiality as natural and needful as the atmosphere.

People take a word and fill it up with certain meanings, such that it constitutes a concept. Now in order to discuss the concept of culture we shall be obliged to say something from recent philosophical arguments about what a concept is and does, and the use we may have or may not have to make of that daunting phrase, 'a conceptual framework', which has been with us since the Enlightenment shed its lights upon the systems of pure reason.

The philosophical support for this view of concept-formation provides a leading lesson in the intellectual method of this book. For in providing this history of our key concept 'culture' we cannot simply start out by discovering its earliest usage. This may be help or hindrance. The *New Oxford Dictionary* lists half a dozen entries, including Matthew Arnold's famous definition, made in 1876, to which we shall turn in a moment. But the early sightings are largely of the term as used in relation to horticulture and the like, even though Thomas More wrote of something being 'to the culture and profit of [people's] minds' as early as 1510.

But it is, as we would expect, in the nineteenth century that 'culture' is attached to the human condition, and not until Arnold's year that we find the usage of 'culture' meaning way of life lived.

These confusing conclusions serve at least to remind us that people may be using a concept before they have a word for it. Even 'using a concept' is not all that straightforward a business, as has been frequently pointed out,[4] and before we can compile a history of the concept of culture, we had better clarify what a concept is, and how we know when we have one. J. L. Austin goes so far as to say that in 'discussion devoted seriously to the question of "origin" and "acquisition" and "formation" of concepts, we are always told either nothing or nonsense'. But as usual in his philosophy, Austin is determined to turn enquiry away from so-called 'universals' (meaning definitions derived from what one may see and touch but then generalized into an abstract 'possession' of the mind). As far as an individual's understanding a concept goes, Austin thought that 'The origin of a concept is commonly admitted to be found, when I can say . . . *with knowledge*, "this is an X" ' (my italics).

Austin was convinced that the history of a word was the history of its uses and, as suggested at the opening of this chapter in connection with some of the vaguer contexts in which 'culture' appears, usage may turn into uselessness. Yet one cannot doubt the usefulness of the concept of culture, nor the fact that all important concepts swim slowly up from murky waters in which one knows there is a precious and useful treasure, but not yet what it is. Quentin Skinner warns us that 'it cannot be a necessary condition for my possessing a concept that I need to understand the correct application of a corresponding term'.[5] His illustration of this is to show how, in his poetry, John Milton was explicitly preoccupied with proving his creative originality, although entirely lacking the word itself to say so. 'Originality' did not enter the English language 'until a century or more after Milton's death'.

Moreover, Skinner continues: nor can it be 'a sufficient condition of my possessing a concept that I understand the correct application of a corresponding term. There is still the possibility (explored by Wittgenstein as well as Kant) that I may believe myself to be in possession of a concept when this belief is in fact mistaken'. This is to claim that one may apply a given term such that one's listeners approve but that the *content* of the concept is so varied that no-one could agree on the meaning in hand. Skinner's examples are 'being' and 'infinity', but he could as well have named 'culture'. He concludes: 'A whole community of language users may be capable of applying these terms with perfect consistency. Yet it might be possible to show that there is simply no concept which answers to any of their agreed usages.'[6] His advice to origin-hunters is that we can discover the advent of a new concept in social intercourse when we observe the development of a particular vocabulary, which is then used to discern and, gradually, to delimit the zone of application in which the concept makes consistent enough sense. (This is not to rule out contradictory senses: many strong concepts, including culture, enclose contradictory meanings.)

This returns us to the early appearances of culture in what we know as the Enlightenment, the unprecedented surge in rationalism and theories of human affairs which took off after 1700 or so. But we should go back to the eighteenth century, however, armed with the truism drawn from Austin and Skinner that in using a concept we are doing just that: *using* it. It is not a neutral theory; it is an evaluative instrument, and carries its special charge. It appeals forcefully to both reason and rhetoric. (It is very hard, for instance, to use 'culture' in disapprobation.)

II

It was Immanuel Kant who first and most clinchingly tackled the mistaken idea that there was a world of material reality out there for which the God-given faculty of pure reason could find an exact linguistic or symbolic mirror (the most dependable set of symbols being taken to be mathematical). Kant pointed out that for the eye to *see* anything, the brain must have learned how to interpret what the eye saw. 'No percepts without concepts' is the label for this insight, but along with it was carried Kant's massive architecture of the mind, according to which we each turn the forms of our mental processes and observations into the foundations of our knowledge. The innate drive to understand provides us 'transcendentally' with the frameworks of comprehension. 'The understanding is itself the lawgiver of nature' is Kant's most famous maxim, followed by 'I must abolish knowledge to make room for belief'. The mind believes, since it has no choice, what it arranges to see.

As befitted a giant of the Enlightenment, Kant placed individual human agency at the very centre of creation. Creation, by this token, was creation of a world for human beings to find inhabitable, and culture, for all those of his contemporaries who began to grasp for such an idea (*not* including Kant among their number), was both form and content of 'conceptual frameworks'.

The Enlightenment, amongst the dazzling beams of which Kant was the brightest, suddenly blazed out and surged across Europe during the second half of the eighteenth century. It was then carried westwards from northern Europe across the Atlantic to strike deep roots among the wealthy

English-, Dutch-, French-, and German-speaking settler-landowners of North America. But like all sun-bright explosions of human thought which illumine, dazzle and sometimes blind human vision, the Enlightenment caused its seers to set off in various directions, eyes fixed on diverse horizons. This coming-of-the-light towards which all intellectual figures of the day turned did not point along a single shining path of progress to the future. It was first a European and then an imperial phenomenon. When this light struck the frontiers of Islamic or Hindu thought, it went out. Its searing potency to burn up the principles and doctrines of theism was felt only in the original continent and subsequently in the geographical regions which Europe came to dominate. It was the Christian God which enlightenment most fatally wounded.

To make sense of this phenomenon, we shall follow it, as did the post-1750 thinkers, along two divergent paths. Each commits us to sketching an early definition of the word 'culture' as it came to assume the status of a coherent, if always disputed and often contradictory, concept. Any such definition, as we shall see, must rest, not on an imaginary distillation of a supposedly incontestable meaning but upon usage. A concept gathers (and loses) substance and essence according to the ways in which it is used. When people protest against the misuse of a concept, they are objecting to incipient changes in its application. This does not mean that such criticism is necessarily mistaken, only that any such objection must be made less on behalf of fixity of meaning, more in the name of what will be lost if the meaning changes.

So when the leaders of Enlightenment thought set off on their sunny road to progress, they did not so much invoke the antique word 'culture' to describe the spirit of an age, but they did configure an account of human being in which a way of thinking, feeling, and speaking would derive itself from a set of data about how the world truly is, allied to a list of precepts as to how it ought to be. This happy combination of thought and action would, they thought, in turn result in such social institutions as would conduce to the good society. Hence the newly emerging force, after the great Revolutions of North America and France, of the idea of a *constitution*.

The word is conventionally taken to be simply legislative in its associations, particularly so given the successful longevity of the American original. But its etymological force is continuous. First, the word names the act of making or forming something; secondly, it names the nature of the thing's construction, the nature of its structure or composition; only thirdly does the *Oxford English Dictionary*[7] acknowledge the political and legal definitions which customarily enclose the word.

When it does so, 'constitution' implicitly signifies the world-making property of this noun. That is to say, the legal rights and political principles set out in the American Constitution themselves devise, shape, and give embodiment to the moral agency of the state whose ideal abstraction forms, structures, and *constitutes* the civic life of the United States of America. It is in this sense that many contemporary human scientists use the word (and its derivative adjective) so frequently; language is by this token itself constitutive of human society. According to what we believe ourselves to mean when we use such key terms as 'reasonable', 'legal', 'promise', 'pay', 'citizen', 'justice', 'contract', 'rights', 'authority', 'evidence', 'believe', 'fact' and 'liberty', so we have thoughts, feel passion and order conduct. Thoughts, passion and conduct are only recognizable as what they are when framed and interpreted by the relevant concepts.

One way of identifying what culture is and means is to say it is the force at work which makes these human behaviours apparent and distinctive. Culture, that is, makes it possible for both the individual performing an action and a spectator interpreting it to characterize the action for what it is, *and* to perform it as such. More particularly, culture makes it possible to distinguish between different versions of the same sort of action, and so attribute it to different human groups. Culture, in other words, teaches us to discriminate between, say, English and Italian courtesies, Argentinian and Japanese art, American and Indonesian management, Chinese and Egyptian medical practice.

These are the fruits of cultural differentiation, and they are also examples of what it is for alternative conceptual systems so to *constitute* or to *realize* action that the idea embodied in that action is made visible in its conduct, movement, line, and sequence. But when the mighty evangelists of human reason set out to enlighten everybody after 1750 or so – when, that is, Voltaire, Goethe, Kant, Montesquieu, Hume, Condorcet, Hegel, Diderot and Berkeley together rode the tidal wave of the new thought which they believed would free humankind from its chains – they did so in the belief in a doctrine and a method which would be universal in application.

This is what is now known as the 'Enlightenment Project'. It taught the basic precepts of science as generalizable to all physical objects, including people. Science, and its practical discoveries and instrumentation under the later heading of technology, represented humankind's incremental victory over nature. Science itself was made possible by the discipline of the detached observation of phenomena and by controlled experimentation designed to test hypotheses intended to explain the phenomena. Such testing found its only absolute validation in the falsification of hypotheses, the only certainty to be found in what was consistently *not* the case (what *is* the case today, as David Hume so cheerfully pointed out, might not be the case tomorrow). Scientific knowledge advanced therefore in a slow series of speculations and tentative confirmations, of conjectures and refutations.[8]

The precepts of scientific method had begun to emerge from its first flowering in late Renaissance Europe. Galileo and Descartes will serve as first prophets of the way of science. They made it possible, by both argument and example, to evade the totalitarian demands of theology. The first displacing of the ancient regime of divine authority and questionless coercion was ratified in Britain when the King was dismissed by the people. It was wholly consistent that this blasphemous and lethal stroke was followed, after the Commonwealth, by the establishment of the Royal Society, an organization, as its first, prompt (1667) historian Thomas Sprat puts it, whose purpose was the 'exantiation of truth' (*sic*), and 'sincere inquiry' to 'remove the rubbish of ages', to effect the separation of poetry from Natural (or Real) Philosophy (by which he meant science), and to pursue the discovery of 'the true channel of Natural Causes and Effects'. All this required the right 'Manner of Discourse' which is to be one of 'primitive purity and shortness . . . a close, naked, natural way of speaking, positive expressions, clear senses; a native easiness; bringing of all things as near the Mathematical plainness as they can'.[9]

The zealots of Enlightenment charged their followers to read Descartes and learn from Galileo, to treat theology as a personal matter among gentlemen and not the object of science, and to do so in prose much influenced, even in France, by Dr Sprat's prescriptions. In this way, society itself would become the object of science; Descartes had written 'Ancient cities that have become large towns in process of time are as a rule badly laid out as compared with those that are laid out by a designer'; the Enlightenment saw the coming on stage of that familiar modern character, the social planner-engineer. Natural philosophy had taught, for instance, Jean-Jacques Rousseau, to discern a common humanity in every manifestation of human being; this emblematic figure, necessarily male, was capitalized as 'Man' and discovered by Rousseau to live trapped in the potentiality of his full humanness, 'born free, but . . . everywhere in chains'.[10]

For these men, freedom was the supreme human value and the condition of human emancipation, science the method with which to supply reason with the knowledge whereby the free, the good society could be designed and assured for the future. When the 'disenchantment of the world' from the superstitions and fancies of heathen darkness was accomplished and, in the savage French Revolutionary joke, the last King strangled with the entrails of the last priest, then Man could enter into the inheritance of freedom and justice.

Such was the picture of the wide road and open gates which would lead to a rational and earthly salvation. The culture of the sacred city of reason would be a clean, well-lit affair; one in which being and becoming would be transparent, serene, rational; in which the streets would be marble-paved and spotless, human relations equable and equal in virtue of the freedoms of reason, and nature herself tamed, provident, and at the unexploited service of man.

Utopias, however, can only be imagined according to the varying historical conditions in which men and women make the effort to do so. The main energies of Enlightenment thinkers were such as to ignore this by now well-known truth about human affairs. The first supreme historicist was Hegel in Prussia, writing his main works as the century turned. But his fellow thinker-reformers were on the whole bent only to the task of cleaning out and cleaning up the old absolutist regimes, sweeping away dead superstitions along with those who promulgated them; in short, ensuring the advent of the society of reason. The main prophet of such reform was the Englishman, Jeremy Bentham, who in a long life astonishing for its compound of detailed and extended academic philosophizing allied to intensely practical proposals for public policy (the French revolutionaries invited him to write their new constitution), devised the principles of utilitarianism (the simple axiom of which was 'the greatest good of the greatest number'), still the foundations of most contemporary political planning.

The conviction of these men was that the good society would be rational in design, egalitarian in justice, comfortable in welfare, and universal in form. Above Bentham rose the towering edifice of Kant's *The Critique of Pure Reason* and his *Answer to the Question: What is Enlightenment?* '[It is] . . . man's emergence from his self-incurred immaturity. Immaturity is the inability to use one's understanding without the guidance of another person . . . Reason has for its object only the understanding and its purposive employment'. Once Kant had systematized 'pure reason', the system could be set to work politics systematically. 'Coherence according to one principle',[11] where the principle in question was systematic reasoning, would order the world for the best, and unselfinterested men like Bentham and James Mill showed with unhesitating clarity how to turn such principle into practice.

III

Opposition to systemic thought had been part of the Enlightenment from the beginning. One could also say that one of the concepts of culture was essential to making the objection. Enlightenment, in commending to humanity One True System, believed itself to have solved the problem of politics. Politics and social method were now coterminous, and once reason had taught this lesson to all human societies, then cruelty, want and war could all be eradicated. The noble science of politics (in the nineteenth-century phrase)[12] would bring paradise on earth and, in so doing, remove the need to hope either for a paradise after life or the redeemer-gardener in charge of it.

The first concept of culture undoes all that from the start. Its prime mover was the German, Johann Gottfried von Herder, contemporary of Kant. Herder initiates that powerful Enlightenment tradition, today a commonplace, which believed in the *un*alikeness of human societies. He criticized the uni-dimensionality of systemic reasoning, unfastened the confident fixities of fact and method, and discovered in the infinite variety of history an unpredictable and contrary physics of human values, the unassimilable particles of which made life as interesting as it turned progress backwards.

The whole tendency of Herder's thought revolves around the concept of culture. The concept is knotted and complex, as we shall see, and he hardly ever uses the word but, as Skinner has taught us, that in no way debars him from deploying the concept, which he does extravagantly.

It is emphatically in Herder's writing that we can see the vocabulary which will eventually distinguish the concept of culture in one range of its applications. (A strong concept gathers to itself its typical idiom.) He uses such a vocabulary freely and passionately, contrived out of the multiple codes of scholarship of which he was, as far as his day permitted, so heterodox a master. He wrote poetry, philosophy, philology; he wrote *about* poetry and literature; like so many men of letters in the Enlightenment, he was much more than a mere dabbler at the frontier of the life sciences, and kept a small laboratory in his house. Like most of his coevals, even when they professed Sprat's principle of 'native leanness' of speech, he wrote volubly, enthusiastically, and with an enormous, impossible inclusiveness.

Herder's main concern[13] is with the sheer variety of human experience and its absolute unamenability to the large and simple classifications of the Enlightenment. His strong nationalism, formed at a time when Germany was still an agglomeration of princedoms dominated by Prussia, led the nation when it *was* a nation into some dead and ugly ends, but in 1770 nationalism was one way of talking about the distinctiveness of cultures. Herder's words for what we would now call 'culture' were 'spirit', 'soul', 'Genius' and 'national character', as located in the 'folk' and made visible, above all, in their arts and crafts. In a rousing and indicative passage

Herder celebrates several key features in the definition of culture: singularity, elusiveness, the totality of a way of life, and, for the scientist of human affairs, the absolute necessity for sympathetic feeling with and for the people:

> How unspeakably difficult it is to convey the particular quality of an individual human being and how impossible it is to say precisely what distinguishes an individual, his way of feeling and living; how different and how individual everything becomes once his eyes see it, once his soul grasps, his heart feels, it. How much depth there is in the character of a single people, which, no matter how often observed (and gazed at with curiosity and wonder), nevertheless escapes the word which attempts to capture it and, even with the word to catch it, is seldom so recognizable as to be universally understood and felt. If this is so, what happens when one tries to master an entire ocean of peoples, times, cultures, countries, with one glance, one sentiment, by means of one single word! Words, pale shadow-play! An entire living picture of ways of life, or habits, wants, characteristics of land and sky, must be added, or provided in advance; one must start by feeling sympathy with a nation if one is to feel a single one of its inclinations or acts, or all of them together.[14]

Herder finds most of his variety in history; the anthropological record was at that date only just beginning to expand with the advent of empire. But the point he makes with historical and linguistic variety is to affirm – almost as an object of moral worship – the self-vindication of alternative ways of life not as stages toward the improvements of the present but as vital, seething, absorbing, and good in themselves for this very liveliness. Pagan societies, which he constantly invokes, like all eighteenth-century scholars, in the venerable forms of classical Greece and Rome, are not mere anticipations of Christendom but brimming with their own kind of beauty and creative vivacity.

He refuses on the one hand to praise the Greeks at the expense of so-called 'Dark Ages', and on the other to work up a state of romantic yearning (*Sehnsucht*) for the splendours of medieval chivalry or gothic art at the expense of a dismal and mediocre present. He is in no way progenitor of those routine culturalist positions which, as W. S. Gilbert put it in one of his wonderful patter songs, prefer 'every century but this and every country but one's own'; his celebrations are for *things as they are* (or were). The sentimentality of idealization and the long complacency of denunciation are, at Herder's best, alike renounced. Talking of the Middle Ages, he writes: 'I am by no means disposed to defend the constant migrations and devastations, the feudal wars, the hordes of monks, the pilgrimages, the crusades. I only want to explain them: to show the spirit that breathed through it all, the seething of human forces.' The breathing spirit, the human seething – this is the content of culture: in this Herder was also a pioneer of what we would now call relativism and which has become an unexamined piety of present-day cultural enquiry.

The doctrine of relativism teaches that all human values are bedded in their own historical and cultural context, and can only have local and transitory meaning. There are therefore no universal values. Herder is a landmark in the establishment of the truths in relativism[15] exactly because he wished to do justice to the exclusiveness and singularity of different ways of life, and to honour these by characterizing the aspects of life which made one people in one epoch wholly themselves: not signposts on their road to progress, not inferior versions of eighteenth-century scholar-gentlemen, nor equivalent representations of the great Enlightenment abstract, Man.

Thus Herder may be transformed into a seer of that latter-day anti-imperialism which detests the march of empire for its obliteration of native culture. Herder, one must conclude, could see all that coming. Isaiah Berlin, his great expositor, tells us that in Herder 'colonial subjugation of native populations, ancient and modern, in and outside Europe, is always represented as being morally odious and as a crime against humanity'.[16]

This is a crucial move in the definition of culture, in that any recognition of the actuality and separateness of a total way of life commits us to respecting it for itself. As I said, the concept enforces the evaluation by virtue of being used. So Herder, good relativist, defends *all* cultures against *any* detractors: on behalf of paganism against Christianity, on behalf of Christianity against atheism, on behalf of the Orient against the Occident.[17] In two arguments, familiar to us, but entirely strange in 1774, Herder interprets the travellers' tales of shamans in exotic lands not as superstitious witch-doctors but as local poets, and the myths they sing[18] not as blindfolds to prevent their audience seeing reality, but as coherent visions of natural being.

In all this vast enterprise, speckled, as one must admit, with incoherence, exaggeration, contradiction, and fulsomeness, Herder does insist upon one paramount value relative to all human necessity. For a people to be a people – Herder is an early and passionate populist – its members must be members one of another. They must *belong* to themselves. Applied to culture, this maxim defines a culture, whatever else it is, as circumscribable and exclusive and, consequently, as ascribing to those members an unmistakable and unshakeable identity.

For Herder the philologist, the ultimate source of membership and identity is language. It was the language of a civilization which grounded its unity, and gave its way of life that identifiable but undefinable patterning and style, as well as shaping its modes of creative expression and its deepest feelings. 'We live in a world we ourselves create,' he wrote, and the maker's instrument is speech. All human beings are by this token makers, and as the great painter Matisse once put it – for our culture-seeking purposes, on behalf of all humankind – 'I am unable to distinguish between the feeling I have for life and my way of expressing it'.[19]

IV

Herder stands in these pages as genius-pioneer of the first notes towards the definition of culture. For all the ardent exaltation of the importance of literature as the highest form of linguistic expression, the features of culture which his concept of it serves to highlight are *totalizing*. Culture is a whole way of life, caught and apprehended by its art and poems, for sure, but manifested all the time in 'the inevitable creativeness of ordinary everyday life'.[20] A culture by this meaning includes only its members and excludes its non-members. It is precious in virtue of its distinctiveness. It is not necessarily going somewhere – towards progress or to the dogs. It *is*, rather than is becoming. Its only given is language and, since language is historical (Herder said that history is like a snowball), a culture develops by way of the thinking inseparable from using language.

To attribute this fairly simple definition to Herder is to ignore the tensions in even his approximation of the idea. For the Enlightenment was nothing if not evangelical, never more so than in its professions of atheism. As a result, even while thinkers alongside Herder commended the variety of innumerable ways of life and contrasted the different spirits of other ages, the might of old Christianity drove them on to find the cultural path leading to the perfectibility of man.[21] Indeed, this is the moment at which paradise is unhitched from the pearly gates of traditional Christian thought, and serious thought is first given to the idea of utopia without a theocracy running things in the name of the Godhead.

One way of thinking such thoughts was provided by Hegel. He was the first to contend that the seeds of new social orders (political and cultural) lay germinating in the forms of the old. Hegel further suggested, unlike Herder, that historical development was and is innately progressive, and that all peoples were tending unevenly (Prussia in the vanguard) towards a realization of the good, because absolutely reasonable, society.

This high-handed vision of the perfectibility of man found a liveable version for itself in a new idea of culture. The rational society would aim to plan a political system which would realize its goals, and the first utilitarians, Bentham and James Mill, proposed as the answer to the question, 'How will the rational polity act to maximise utility and welfare?', their pet calculus, 'the greatest good of the greatest number', where 'greatest good' meant the happiest distribution of material welfare: food, shelter, health, fuel.

No-one, almost two hundred years later, can scoff at such sums. But the objection made by James Mill's son, John Stuart, is completely irrefutable. John Stuart Mill laid the main charge against Bentham's utilitarianism, when he wrote that Bentham simply could not recognize that 'Man is a being capable of pursuing spiritual perfection as an end', because

Bentham's conception of human existence is constrained entirely by his debit-and-credit ledger-book of life in which the only entries are under 'pleasure' and 'pain'.[22] 'Spiritual perfection' is not a phrase to be used without a trace of embarrassment in the present, but it introduces that other realm of meaning latent in the gospel of culture from the start.

'Bentham committed the mistake of supposing that the business part of human affairs was the whole of them',[23] Mill wrote, and then gives Bentham, as well he might, all credit for the greatness of what he had done in this field: '[he] swept away the accumulated cobwebs of centuries . . . untied knots which the efforts of the ablest thinkers, age after age, had only drawn tighter.' But the deadliest criticism is made more personally in Mill's most famous single quotation. In the *Autobiography*[24] he recounts the deep emotional crisis which struck him down when, with the remarkable honesty and courage which so characterized Mill, he faced his father's and Jeremy Bentham's system for society with the devastating question, ' "Suppose that all your objects in life were realized; that all the changes in institutions and opinions which you are looking forward to could be completely effected at this very instant: would this be a great joy and happiness to you?" And an irrepressible self-consciousness distinctly answered, "No!".' A society run entirely on his parent's theory of business reasonableness would, Mill saw, be a null and deathly place.

Mill's medicine for his breakdown, as given in the *Autobiography*, was to read Wordsworth's poetry. Here, in perhaps his second most famous passage, he uses the word 'culture' itself to indicate the redemptive power of poetry for feelings frozen by the pedagogic march of instrumental reason. Wordsworth's poems, Mill found,

> seemed to be the very culture of the feelings which I was in quest of. In them I seemed to draw from a source of inward joy, of sympathetic and imaginative pleasure . . . which had no connection with struggle or imperfection, but would be made richer by every improvement in the physical or social condition of mankind. From them I seemed to learn what would be the perennial sources of happiness when all the greater evils of life shall have been removed.[25]

It is an odd way to put it, that Wordsworth's poetry 'seemed to *be* the very culture of the feelings', and the passage, plainly heartfelt and fluidly written, is not without its contradictions. 'Culture' in this sense and at that date meant the slow attentions of human labour as given to natural cultivation. Poetry could not *be* that culture without some kind of human intervention, nor is it quite consistent of Mill to say that poetry stands above the struggle of life but may still be enriched by human progress.

Nonetheless, what comes over here is Mill's invocation of great poetry as an exalted realm of culture, and this is the other meaning of the word and content of the concept which lends its semantic structure such high tension. This meaning is also there from the outset in the work of a German contemporary of Herder's.

Friedrich Schiller, the nearest equivalent to a German Shakespeare, author of a tremendous and exhilarating range of poetic-historical dramas from *The Robbers* and *William Tell* to *Maria Stuart* and *Wallenstein*, wrote in 1795 a series of *Letters on the Aesthetic Education of Man* which makes a more-or-less direct identification of *Kultur* and the arts, especially literature. Not only that. Schiller aligns *Kultur* and the German noun, *Bildung*, usually translated as 'education' but 'formation' would perhaps be closer (at its most literal, *Bild* means a 'picture', as in 'self-imaging').

The continued force of the idea of a civilization as opposed to barbarity is indispensable to the very notion of human betterment, let alone of the good society. In the present state of world politics much is made of the phrase 'the civilized nations' and anybody would wish most urgently to be a member of one of them. The trouble is that the moment you hear the phrase, you also hear the warblings of propaganda and the arrogance of class.

These conflicting meanings are probably ineradicable from any strongly evaluative and nobly moral-political term. They are certainly present in the idea of art, as they are in that of democracy; the rich ambiguities of 'nobility', 'virtue' (with its etymological root in *vir*, the Latin for a male), 'liberty' and 'fraternity', all bear witness to the *contested*[26] nature of almost all the most important and high-minded of our moral and political ideals.

Schiller was an Enlightenment didact all-through; he believed in the emancipatory precepts of freedom and equality, as well as in the liberating propensity of the new reasoning as applied to society; he was committed to the certainty of human improvement, and was among the first of those who countered the old conservative objection that human beings were determinately sinful, habitually indolent, and congenitally unimprovable, by appealing to literature and art as enshrining the innate human potentiality for goodness and beauty. So Schiller wrote: 'Every individual human being, one may say, causes within him, *potentially and prescriptively*, an ideal man, the archetype of a human being, and it is his life's task to be, through all his changing manifestations, in harmony with the unchanging unity of this ideal.'[27]

We can attribute to Schiller the original Romantic identification of the artist in every human being, and each individual life as containing the perfect work of art the individual should strive to make of it. Schiller may also be credited with launching the idea of culture as meaning high art, and high art (whether or not the product of incomparable genius) as the domain of the ideal, because imaginary, account of how life could one day be. As Schiller sees it, culture has curative properties: by embodying the ideal, it provides a criterion for criticism of life as it actually is.

This meaning moves one part of the concept decisively away from and, at times, in opposition to the other. This is what it is to be a 'contested concept'. Culture-as-ideal-form criticizes cultures-as-the-teeming-ways-of-daily-lives in many different countries. Art the-mirror-held-up-to-life becomes art the-lamp-held-up-to-light-the-way-forward.

Schiller added to this meaning the dimension of playfulness. Art (and culture) would make possible that fulfilment of human potentiality impossible in the work of a civilization preoccupied by trade, exchange and commercial life in general. Hence, for Schiller, the dictum that 'the human being is only fully human when at play'.[28] Culture is then the nonpurposeful, the imaginative, the anti-instrumental realm and fount of unproductive play.

V

Herder and Schiller, writing in the minor princedoms dominated by pre-German Prussia, announce in their contrastive
ways the imminent victory of the *Aufklärung*. By the time
John Stuart Mill faces up to his breakdown in 1834, the
French Revolution is over and done with, the centre of both
political and cultural action has moved to Britain, and their
blazing hope for a utopian future, which had led the intelligentsia along the road to enlightenment, found itself at the
gates of the new industrial city.

They did not like what they saw and reached for the
weapon of culture with which to assault it. As they did so,
the meanings of the concept whose origins we have followed
began to solidify and to attach themselves by general usage
to the word itself.

At first, in the clamorous argument since referred to as 'the
condition of England debate', commentators largely used
'civilization' and 'culture' as interchangeable terms. Either
one indicated that civility of public life which is embodied in
a society's learning, entertainment, manners, and legislation,
as well as in its systems of production and its conventions of
exchange. If all these customs and practices were civilized,
then the citizens would possess culture and be formed in
cultivation.

Mill, as we saw, nominated Bentham as the great philosopher of successful social rationalization. In a brilliant insight,
which captures in a single opposition those representative
thinkers trying to enclose in a single theory the multiple currents of the century, he counterposes to Bentham the poet
Coleridge. Coleridge's famous dictum, 'men ought to be
weighed and not counted', similarly catches up the debate as
a struggle between incommensurable kinds of enquiry:
Benthamites count; Coleridgeans weigh. We might rewrite
the same struggle as between politics (counting) and culture
(weighing).

Coleridge's 'weighing' goes rather beyond mere avoir-
dupois. It is more a matter of weighing up, of a judicious,
intuitive, interpretative, sympathetic, and (in part) physical
responsiveness to others in all their totality and (what came

later to be called, in an important coinage) in their 'alterity' or 'otherness'. Herder's *Einfühlung* (now translated as 'empathy') and, a century or so later, Max Weber's *Verstehen*[29] (readily translated as 'understanding') are both surely present in Coleridge's methodical admonition, and the object of all these references is culture.

Coleridge is our first metaphysician of method in cultural enquiry. But by the time England approached her keenest political crisis since the Civil War, cultural enquiry was inseparable from political polemics, and culture itself had knotted together its threefold, contradictory meanings: culture as those presences, structures and formations moving through society which make for civility and civilization; culture as the specialized precipitation of these presences into what counts as high art; culture as the whole congeries of expressive customs and practices, the materials which comprise them, the passions which form and inform them, for good and ill.[30] By 1848, accordingly, culture was a blunt instrument in the waging of a new kind of social struggle between the different classes created and allocated by the mighty and unprecedented cities of industrialism.

'Industrialism' was a word coined by Thomas Carlyle although, like 'culture', the concept had been in formation for some decades. Carlyle was an early prophet of the coming class war; he published in 1829 his long essay, 'Signs of the Times' in which he identifies his day as 'the Age of Machinery', its absolute frame of reference as 'the cash-nexus' or the 'Religion of Profit', indicting its disregard of the importance of people's inner lives, its eradication of 'Moral Force', its brutal preference for 'mere political arrangements' over questions of culture.[31]

Carlyle inaugurated a long tradition in British society of criticism of blind and mechanical industrialism and profiteering, but he was himself far from being a reactionary opponent of the Enlightenment's ideal of progress. He put the rousing question: 'Is the condition of the English working people wrong; so wrong that rational working men cannot, will not, and even should not rest quiet under it?' The concept of capitalism was not yet available to him, but that of democracy certainly was. What Carlyle was able to see and name with a grand rhetorical force were those drives in culture conceived of as his nation's way of life, which would work to destroy that culture conceived of as 'the best which has been thought and said in the world'.

This famous definition belongs to Matthew Arnold and is not voiced until he published his great classic, *Culture and Anarchy*, in 1869. But it is important to notice that Carlyle, like Arnold, was anxious to nourish the present with the best of the past. Both men recognized the reactionary repulsiveness of what Raymond Williams in our own day scornfully identified as 'the long sighing of the just; the mature, sad consciousness of non-intervention'.[32] So when Carlyle turned to celebrate the living and exemplary culture of a long-dead monastic community in Catholic and medieval England, he did so with a pedagogue's eye on what it could teach England in her crisis of the 1840s. He rediscovered in St Albans and its abbot in the Middle Ages the necessary and sufficient conditions of living culture. Perhaps Carlyle may be counted the first of the Romantics to tell his country, in his stirring, pamphleteering way, that progress would turn to regression and decadence unless it held onto those forms of life which civilize people *of themselves*, which conduce to goodness and virtue because of the smallest details of everyday exchange.

In Carlyle's picture of the St Albans monastery, culture lives in the pious and gregarious lives of the brothers, their serene and unreflexive dedication of their lives to a larger significance than their individual goodness, easy balance between worship, study of the sacred texts, practical (and effortful) husbandry, robust but simple gastronomy, and in all these things as defining and shaping their responsibility towards the town and the peasant life around it.

Naturally, there is plenty of idealization in this contented fresco of English life a long way from Carlyle's present. But although Carlyle initiated a genre of wistful remembrances and reproachful nostalgia, his purposes were immediate. They were to criticize the unspeakably commercial present, with its filthy factories and starving work-people, for a lack of the conditions of a culture refusing profit, constricting power, affirming community. Such circumstances once obtained; they were recoverable.

We can give Carlyle the credit for first joining culture to community. We hand to William Morris the distinction of joining culture to politics. In his great fable of How Things Ought to Be, *News from Nowhere*,[33] Morris describes his communist utopia in terms comparable to Carlyle's St Albans of sixty years previously. Here, too, work is fulfilling, production cleansed, social relations equal because classless, and the beauty of an unexploited nature in graceful harmony with the truthfulness and loveliness of domestic furniture and adornment everywhere to be found.

By 1890, of course, it was clear to Morris that, in order to achieve such a cultural order, political revolution was unavoidable. Morris had absorbed Marx but without losing his hold on either the detail of everyday life or the need to ensure that the political power of the state was confined by cultural value.

Morris had grasped more clearly than any of his contemporaries[34] a lesson urgently needing to be relearned by the millenarians of today: that culture, whatever it is, cannot be planned but will have its way; that it both expresses and forms the hearts and minds of men and women; but that it is subordinate to (as well as insubordinate towards) politics, and that politics is the only instrument we have to turn hope into endeavour, desire into actuality. As he wrote with hot scorn: 'In the thirty years during which I have known Oxford more damage has been done to art ... by Oxford "culture" than centuries of professors could repair ... Those coarse brutalities of "light and leading" make education stink in the nostrils of thoughtful persons, and are more likely than is socialism to drive some of us mad.'[35] It was, Morris said, the helots of the bourgeois class and its damnable 'culture' which were destroying history while purporting to teach literature. Morris in his turn drew upon the divided meanings of the concept held within the structure of the word 'culture'; he turned his passionate and eloquent detestation upon what the commercial classes had made of the culture he saw about him, and he summoned up the powerful ghost of a redemptive art. For 'the cause of Art is the cause of the people ... One day we shall win back Art, that is to say the pleasure of life; win back Art again to our daily labour.'[36] And, most moving of all, 'It is the province of art to set the true ideal of a full and reasonable life before him, a life to which the perception and creation of beauty shall be as necessary to man as his daily bread.'[37]

The middle class (while counting himself a member of it) was for him as frequently dislikeable as it is now. For it protects itself with its money and its privileges from seeing what the commercial life it lives off does to other people whom it dispatches to live in 'slums, the squalor of a factory country', amidst drunkenness and brutalization. 'Culture' had and has done these things, and Morris's plea was not, as he said, on behalf of art, 'but for the lives of men'. If those lives were to be made good again, they might have to endure a certain temporary bareness as the love of art required the sweeping away of the unendurable shams of art which constituted so much of Victorian culture. (No-one can say – can they? – that Morris is no longer a relevant writer).

VI

We begin to approach the extraordinary explosiveness of the concept of culture. For by these tokens, as endorsed by Morris, when I encounter a piece of your culture, it will tell me what to think of you, and, in a polite and politic way, I may say what that is and judge you accordingly. No wonder that culture is, as Marxists say, a site of struggle, or as we might more familiarly put it, a touchy subject, and quite certain to be quarrelled over.

William Morris picked his quarrels carefully. His was with the ruling class and with what it had made of the promise of happiness held out by art on behalf of a common culture. Culture spoke of, to and for the soul of a people, certainly; but if it were appropriated by rulers and made to speak only of money, it became an abomination. Art, as Morris said, 'is the cause of the people' and will only speak well on their behalf when it belongs to them. Politics draws its figure upon the ground of culture; one cannot be seen without the other.

In taking this position, Morris sets himself against Matthew Arnold, the best-known cultural theorist in British intellectual history and certainly a paramount influence in the confection of our key concept as it exfloriates throughout the nineteenth century. The two men may be counterposed as advocates of culture on the one hand (Arnold) and politics on the other (Morris), while both remained intensely aware of the other's weight in the balance. When Morris wrote this – 'if art . . . is to live and not die . . . it must be of the people, for the people, by the people; it must understand all and be understood by all' – he was writing a political manifesto on behalf of culture. When Arnold wrote in the conclusion to his mighty work, 'This [the doctrine of the redemptive power of culture] is the *social* idea, and the men of culture are the true apostles of equality', he was in contrast setting out a cultural bill of rights on behalf of the polity.

Culture and Anarchy is culture's first sacred book and, like most sacred books, not much read any longer. If one turns over its opening pages it is a surprise to hear again that excellently high-minded eloquence and to reflect that, for all its unfashionability, Arnold's combination of seriousness and combativity makes a much more immediate appeal than the book's reputation allows. Of course, to find an early definition of culture as, in the famous phrases, 'a pursuit of our total perfection by means of getting to know . . . the best which has been thought and said in the world' is more than a little daunting, even for modern-day self-improvers, and downright ridiculous to contemporary relativism. But fairmindedness remains a value with a good deal of life to it none the less, and anybody with this book in their hands is not only pretty likely to agree with Arnold that one's life depends for 'solidity and value' on the company of the writers that one keeps, but that if one allows 'a fresh and free play of the best thoughts upon one's stock notions and habits, one has got culture'.

Arnold, devout Anglican, had the intellectual honesty to see that the established church in Europe was losing its authority as a guide to daily conduct, as well as its radiance in lighting believers to ultimate truth. Dutifully shaped by the high-minded absolutes of his public-school headmaster-father, he offered as the guide to, and shaping spirit of, social and personal redemption, 'the study of perfection' implicit in the greatest writings of the traditional syllabus of European universities since the Renaissance. Thereafter, culture in the Arnoldian sense contracts itself to a national literature. Arnold, schools inspector and son of a schoolteacher, understood that the best way to play freshly and freely with ideas was in the immediately attractive forms of poetic and prose narrative.

Put like that, Arnold's culture is the same as Mill's: 'the very culture of the feelings' which Mill found in the beauties of Wordsworth's poetry and which rescued him from breakdown. Arnold's point is, however, more conscientiously educational. Religion's sources of spiritual irrigation are drying up; great poetry and its embodiment of high-mindedness allied to powerful feeling can be substituted for them to flow in one clear current through all the people. But Arnold's culture is not merely a guide to conduct for those faltering in religious belief. It is a secular church militant, and its satanic enemy is called 'anarchy'.

When Arnold sees anarchy, he finds not political meaninglessness (the usual meaning of 'anarchy') but a culture without standards. Picking up the language of Coleridge and Carlyle quite consciously (this is how a concept – as it was put earlier – binds its meanings about itself like strands on a rope), Arnold says that 'the whole civilization is . . . mechanical and external'. Its empire-builders are in Arnold's most famous coinage 'Philistines', and in a twist as typically English as it could be French, Arnold repudiates philistinism not by argument but by condescension.

It is at this point that we can say snobbery is decisively added to our pet concept, and continues to 'supercharge' its contemporary meaning, for

> Culture says: Consider these people, then, their way of life, their habits, their manners . . . observe the literature they read, the things which give them pleasure, the words which come forth out of their mouths, the thoughts which make the furniture of their minds; would any amount of wealth be worth having with the condition that one was to become just like these people by having it?[38]

One way of measuring a degree of social progress since Arnold wrote this would be the recognition that a majority of people would recoil from its supercilious tone, the confident presumptuousness about the lives and thoughts of so many other people.

The twentieth century provided a number of violent and horrific versions of an answer to this question which presage ill for the twenty-first, and may make us feel better about Arnold's attitude. For those total theories-and-practices of society usually called 'totalitarian' set themselves to put down money worship, provincial small-mindedness, doing as one damn well pleases, and all the other disagreeable manifestations of philistinism in the name of a morally excellent system of politics-become-culture. With their grand parades and spectacular shows of military power and collective feeling, both Fascism and Stalinism held out the prospect of dissolving bourgeois self-seekingness and acquisition in the larger good of national identity, whether German 'blood and soil', Italian rediscovery of a fake Romanness, or Russian superman proletarians marching into the future behind tanks and tractors. In 2001, another local totalitarianism put on its own minor but appalling spectacle in order to prove that Islamic believers also detested the bourgeoisie, and would kill themselves in order to destroy the hateful pinnacles of world trade, the domination of the globe by godless American money.

In the face of these monstrous aesthetics, Arnold's culture, defined by him so variously and so vaguely, retains its dazzling potency, a characteristic it shares with the imagery of Platonism and Christianity, which can fill the gaze of humankind. For as the philosopher Wittgenstein asks, 'is it even always an advantage to replace an indistinct picture by a sharp one? Isn't the indistinct one often exactly what we need?'[39]

Arnold's is certainly, in Wittgenstein's words, 'a concept with blurred edges'. There is no doubt, however, that Arnold's culture serves to pick out those features of life which either include the arts or provide their foundations, especially of a moral sort. He empties into the enormous capacity of the concept its power to help the human race 'make endless additions to itself', to achieve 'endless expansion of its powers . . . endless growth in wisdom and beauty'.[40] The generality of these terms does not detract from their noble seriousness and attraction to anyone today who, however averse to the phrase 'these people', still finds the hate-filled hypocrisy of the yellow press disgusting, or the delirious worship of manic celebrity on television demeaning and contemptible.

Arnold's culture continues to stand in fierce and intransigent hostility to that concept of culture which expresses itself in young British women shown on a TV holiday programme bawling drunkenly outside a Spanish bar, 'What do we want? Williees . . . How do we want them? Haaard.' It is almost too coarse a jolt to follow these little charmers with Arnold's addition of 'sweetness and light'[41] to his 'pursuit of perfection', a phrase he took from Swift and by which he meant such abstracts as 'beauty and harmony', 'increased life, increased sympathy', something far greater than 'the blessedness of the franchise, of the wonderfulness of [our society's] own industrial performances'.

Arnold prescribes his wholesome medicine explicitly in opposition to political manifestos. What he refers to as 'Jacobinism' is the political zeal to work up indignation against the past, to renovate wholesale, to apply 'black and white doctrines for elaborating . . . a rational society for the future',[42] all of which exactly match later totalitarianisms. His culture therefore has no programme; it is a secular version of the Anglican catechism's 'inward and spiritual grace', it seeks constantly to *criticize*, but only by way of indicating how far matters of fact fall short of fulfilment. When Arnold's many enemies among the Philistines deride the man of culture for his uselessness, Arnold offers the classic, ironclad, and irrefutable justification of intellectual life, that 'where bitter envying and strife are, there is confusion and every evil work', that

> the great men [let us add, as a safe measure of actual progress since then, 'great women' also] of culture are those who . . . have laboured to divest knowledge of all that was harsh, uncouth, difficult, abstract, professional, exclusive; to humanise it, to make it efficient outside the clique of the cultivated and learned, yet still remaining the *best* knowledge and thought of the time, and a true source, therefore, of sweetness and light.[43]

By such a token, Arnold cannot escape (and does not wish to) committing culture to the care of the good society's self-education. For all his very strong sense of his own Englishness,[44] Arnold is sharply aware of and eloquently outspoken about the truth that Victorian Britain is a pretty shabby version of the good society. Beside the stifling omnipresence of the Philistines loom the self-satisfied 'Barbarians', Arnold's name for the aristocracy, convincingly damned by him. He accuses the class of a culture (and here Arnold uses the word to designate a way of life but adds 'to call it by that name' by way of indicating how far it falls short of the ideal) which is 'mainly exterior'; it consists principally in 'outward gifts and graces, in looks, manners, accomplishments', and he concludes by finding in it, as well he might, a lack of *soul*.[45]

Faced by his grisly trinity, Barbarians, Philistines and a working-class Populace 'wholly occupied . . . with the things of itself and not its real self, with the things of the State and not the real State', Arnold can only commit his conception of culture to the various forms of self-education conceivable to the self-broadcasting of his society.

Hence both the vague but pervasive optimism which so strongly colours his concept of culture, and the admonitory tinge the word carries for us as a result. Arnold's culture, framed out of his inheritance from Schiller and Coleridge, Carlyle and Wordsworth, but given practical application and polemical edge by his own and his father's educational ardour, remains embedded in our contemporary and contested meaning. His culture, once realized, will be good for us; before that transfiguration, it is immanent in the actual world as something of which, if we attend to it, we shall one day be capable; it therefore identifies actual and noble possibilities in our lives, the best that we might truly bring to birth, and it consequently equips us with the criteria and weaponry of self-criticism. It connects desire with actuality, and provides a measure of the gap between the two.

VII

By the end of the nineteenth century, therefore, culture is a concept armed and weighty enough to take on politics. But it had, as we see, a very confused provenance and lent itself to the rhetoric of entirely opposed political arguments. Speaking roughly, we can say that there is a convergence of reference between the two words, 'civilization' and 'culture', as we approach the modern era which opened with such a bang in 1914. They also carry with them strong associations with community and with art.

At about this juncture, culture became what it remains: protean, enormous, inclusive, bloodily disputed. This is therefore the moment to insist on its one reassuring quality: its *ostensivity*. That is to say, we can only be sure what we are talking about when we can display it for inspection. This seems to be the easiest response to those who ask for definitions of culture or those who complain that they never know what theorists of culture are talking about. Nothing is dismissable for the culturalist. The casual observer asks, 'Why bother with that shit?', but the cultural archaeologist, down on his knees in the site of five-thousand-year-old latrines, takes up the fossils to discover in their petrifaction the cuisine, the physical strength, the mortality and the crops on the allotment of the stone-age original whose morning dump he holds in reverent tongs. Culture may be a vague enough concept but breakfast, fatal illness and crop yields are not. Culture, that is to say, is to be found in the *signs* of human action and the ideas that action embodies.[46] You can only find it insofar as you can interpret what people are doing when they express it. It is *embedded* in the contexts and settings of everyday life, and made visible in the *irreducible* nature of social exchange and interaction.

This way of expressing things was scarcely an option at the moment at which social science began. For Bentham, James Mill and the French social theorist Auguste Comte, the science of human affairs was a strictly factual, methodically empirical, and reductively computational practice. Their allies in the new, headlong and exceedingly self-righteous business of capitalism took a similar view. Hence culture, in the high-toned sense of Carlyle and Matthew Arnold, took on (as we have noted) an oppositional charge which always placed it in a critical location *vis-à-vis* both social science and the political economy which produced it.[47]

Art, as the precipitate of culture, became charged in the same way and so, gradually, was the concept's third zone of application, whereby the whole life of a single society could be circumscribed as its culture. For on the one hand, the new scientists of industrial society, shown the way by Bentham and Comte, set about devising the techniques for the regulation of production, the legislation of behaviour, the instruction in skills, and the very ordering and classifying of passion and action[48] on behalf of all their fellow workers. On the other hand, however, a mixed and argumentative collection of critics set their faces against such an incarceration exactly because they could see and feel, with a mixture of horror and delight, just how intense, throbbing and vivid was the vulgarity of the way of life produced by the new industrialization, and the exhilarating, revolting city in which it thrived.

So it was by way of the monstrous and magical life of the street – in Paris, London, New York, Chicago, Vienna, Rome, Berlin, St Petersburg – that the concept of culture took on such a multi-coloured substance, and at the same time such a divided selfhood. The mighty novelists – Dickens, of course, along with Proust, Henry James, Tolstoy, Musil and several dozen others – saw the city's magic and its monstrosity as inseparable.

For its hostile critics, mostly members of a class which leaves town for the weekend, urban culture, irresistible as it is, debauches those who stay and estranges those who do not. The culture of redemption is then to be found elsewhere, by the oasis of community. This is the last departure of the century and it is, tellingly, to find such redemption far afield, in the territories of empire. Culture, long apostrophized as the source of human perfection, splits in two. The residue is found in the Cities of the Plain of Modernity: an unmistakably vital but frightful way of life. The distillation is to be found up in the hills or on the other side of the world in the self-enclosed lives of what are then depictable – literally so in the example of Gauguin's wonderful idealizations of the natives of Tahiti – as utopias.

The reality of utopia is elsewhere, whether in history or geography. Ruskin's Gothic Venice, Henry Adams's Mont St Michel and Chartres, Carlyle's St Albans, Morris's shining Nowhere set beside a Silver Thames in the perfect communist future, Saint-Simon's and Fourier's Golden Age of the Future, Marx's post-revolutionary egalitarianism, are all grasped and imagined as *beyond politics*.[49] Insofar as these are good societies, politics will have done its work and dissolved into the perpetuity of culture. Thus politics is struggle and culture is harmony.

This is the last dimension of meaning which completes and complicates the concept in readiness for the twentieth century. Its advent may be said to mark the first anthropological moment. Anthropology is no doubt a science of human affairs but it has of late acknowledged what has been the argument throughout this chapter, that the concepts deployed in human enquiry are not only 'contested', ambiguous in meaning and enclosing the contradictions of differing usages, they are also heavy with judgement, past and incipient. When E. B. Tylor published his pioneering book *Primitive Culture* in 1871, the very title announced a judgement: that those who were once called 'savages' and were still called 'primitives' had a true culture of their own, that it was coterminous with community and exclusive of the outward world, and that – as anthropology developed – primitive culture taught its peoples a dignity, a self-reliance, and a narrative of living-and-dying that was untouched by the monstrosities of industrial modernity, and served as a moral lesson in the nobility with which they lived in a serene, unexploitative relation to nature.

Living in culture, primitive peoples had no politics. That was what made them primitives. They had a social structure – how could they not? – and every detail of culture, their weapons, their cooking, their kinship and their ceremonies confirmed and expressed that structure as giving their lives their enviable unity.

Anthropology was, no doubt, the science devised for the regulation of those peoples subordinated by empire.[50] It was also the critical method of those alienated from but academically employed by the imperial powers. The first explorer-anthropologists were no hired mouths of empire. Homesick and home-estranged, they saw the violent clash of old and new cultures, and the flow of blood and money which followed. The professional anthropologists followed the same trail, looking for culture, taking it with them in cameras, safari jackets, folding chairs and beds, wicker baskets, bell tents, revolvers and rifles.

Anthropology appropriates culture for its own; literary criticism tries to pull it back; novelists fill it up with all kinds of clutter from domestic life; political revolutionaries and reactionaries subject it to Five and Fifty Year Plans. By 1914 culture is become indispensable to theory, and Theory is the new muse of the totalitarian century.

2
Culture and Politics

It was John Stuart Mill's genius to see that, from the very beginning of modernity, there was an irresolvable struggle between the rationalist planners and their hopes for a universal enlightenment, and the romantic individualists and *their* hopes for a democracy of the feelings. This was the fight as Mill fixed it between Bentham and Coleridge or, as we might say, between politics and culture.

It was the signal contribution of novelists during the nineteenth century to 'a science of human affairs' (in R. G. Collingwood's great phrase) to do three things, none better than Dickens. The first was to pursue the sweeping currents of mighty historical forces into the making of individual lives. The second was to intuit and confront the centrality of the new industrial city in the shaping of all human life and in ordering the news of the world. The third was to invent a method of observation and recording which would identify the human *values* – those fierce condensations of meaning – symbolized in human action. The novelist sees the symbols dancing in the whirl and bustle of social life, and finds in them the best and the worst of what any given section of humankind is thinking.

You can see this way of discerning, feeling and understanding emerge in the European novel across the century.

You can see its authors experimenting with the method in diaries such as those of the Goncourt brothers or, supremely, in the many volumes of his travel writing by Henry James. When James considers Venice,[1] he finds its culture in the way in which 'art and life seems so interfused and, as it were, consanguineous'.[2]

That terrific din, which James and Dickens in their different ways sorted, dramatized, and judged, becomes aware of itself as politics. The noise of a society's conversation may be culture, as Michael Oakeshott suggested,[3] but it becomes, he continued, 'the greatest but also the most hardly sustained of all the accomplishments of mankind'. The difficulty is the unavoidable presence of barbarism in all culture. Insofar as the conversation of culture sustains itself in human exchange, changing minds and fastening on facts, it becomes capable of self-reflection. When it does so, it speaks politics.

Putting things this way is to paraphrase the coming to power of public opinion. Before public opinion became a key force in politics, ruling classes exercised their leadership, exacted obligation and compelled obedience by the mixed rules of divinity, law, and violence. In the centuries-long debate which led to the foundation and institution of the State instead of the absolute monarch, a key space was gradually defined and opened in which the myth of public opinion so essential to the democratic idea could flourish.[4]

Public opinion, varied and hard to determine as it is, then becomes the self-consciousness of a culture and the energy of politics without which no political will may be formed and directed. Culture may be 'the hum and buzz of implication' in human activity and exchange, but insofar as it becomes determinate, it transforms itself into opinions.

This preamble is important if we are to grasp the peculiar significance of culture in the politics of what Eric Hobsbawm[5] calls 'the short twentieth century' and which opened in 1914. At that point culture was, as we have seen, pregnant with possibility but still only incipient in social theory. It contained its triple meanings: as social ideal; as that ideal concentrated in the expressive arts; as a way of life distinctive to a particular society and visibly expressed in its social symbolism. The coming to irresistible prominence of different sections of public opinion attributable to different social classes turned culture into a new political weapon. The political leaders who were quickest to understand this were, as one would expect, the revolutionaries.

One sees this innovation at its earliest and simplest in the pamphleteering of Leon Trotsky, most vulgarly in the public theatre of Benito Mussolini, and most theoretically in the writings of Antonio Gramsci.

II

Trotsky wrote *Literature and Revolution*[6] even while commanding the Red Army during the terrible conflagration of the Russian civil war, which drifted to defeat for the Whites and their half-hearted allies in Britain and the USA, in 1921. A writer of extraordinary power and intelligence, and an equally ruthless politician, Trotsky understood that the imaginative reach and moral vision of his nation's culture was something which had somehow to be swung behind the purposes of the revolution if it was to succeed. He also understood that the amazing cultural resources of his nation and of the intelligentsia who were its custodians had been kept aloof from the revolution even while sympathetic to its aims. Further, he could also see that the ferment of creative work launched by the poets Alexander Blok and Vladimir Mayakovsky in the yellow blouses which were the uniform of the Futurist movement was, for all its vivacity and clamour, politically undirected and cognitively unintelligible to most people and to the people as a whole. Trotsky heard his fellow revolutionaries of an intellectual persuasion dismissing the art, architecture, and literature of the previous century as bourgeois and therefore contemptible, fit only for the dustbin of history. He riposted: 'To reject art as a means of picturing and imaging knowledge because of one's opposition to the contemplative and impressionistic bourgeois art . . . – the passive realism and dreamy symbolism of the Chekhov school – is to strike from the hands of the class which is building a new society its most important weapon.'[7] Culture, for Trotsky, belongs to the utopian realm; it is synonymous with art (and with architecture, *the* political art) and serves the best life of the present as an account of how the better life of the future could be – better because freer, more just, more equal, more fulfilled.

To this noble end, politics would have to re-imagine culture and, in so doing, take it out of the hands of its then owners, the bourgeoisie. Criticism would become creation in that, in a drastic revaluation of old literature on behalf of new rulers, the moral vision of the old masters would shine through the eyes of the proletariat, so that they might see the celestial city of the future on earth. Hence the title chosen by the new poets and painters for their movement, 'the Futurists'.

It was the Bolsheviks after their coup in 1917 who first and most brilliantly planned for the unplannable zest of culture and art to be bent to explicitly political purposes. Not just public opinion but public passion was both behind and all around them, and, until Stalin's deathly hand fell on art and killed culture after 1928 or so, Russia offers a glowing, extremely short-lived example of art and politics in harmony and expressing something pure and simple in the best culture of the time.

To generalize, we can say that after 1928 ideology organized culture. It did so in the two powers in which Fascism won its one-generation victory, thereby teaching us an opaque but painful lesson in the limitedly redemptive powers of culture. In Italy, Mussolini, a man of some culture, assumed power in 1921 with an immediate, intuitive understanding of the symbolism which would fasten Italian cultures (with their great differences between the Communist car- and textile-workers of the north and the devout peasants of the *mezzogiorno*) together: Vatican ceremony, Risorgimento ardour, and Roman imperial history would be united in a new, technologically sumptuous spectacle. With the daring and energy of, it must be said, a genius of mass vulgarity, Mussolini chose the architects, designers, musicians and impresarios of such a spectacle, who were to assemble a living culture for his politics within a handful of years.

The railway station, the motor car, the aeroplane spoke alike of Fascist success in conquering the time and space to come and driving straight over the objections of the past. The massive façades of the central stations of Rome and Milan, the gleaming streamlining of Bugatti and Alfa Romeo boastfully declared party, state and nation as riding into an impregnable future. The sign of the *fasces*, the riding boots and breeches, the ceremonial swords and huge, beautiful flags and banners, the propinquity of great dictator and Holy Mother Church, all spoke for the continuity of classical and imperial Rome with contemporary government. Augustus, Virgil, Michelangelo and the Medici, together with Garibaldi were each conscripted in a new cultural politics.

Culture into propaganda was an ideological transformation. Long before the 1920s, in their subsequently famous notebooks entitled *The German Ideology*, Karl Marx and Friedrich Engels had noted the tautology that 'in every age the ideas of the ruling class are the ruling ideas'.[8] Once the new coinage, 'ideology', was in busy circulation, it was easy to launch the industry of propaganda and to use art as the readiest medium in which to dramatize and outline the ideas of any class, new or old, offering to rule in the name of those same ideas.

The epoch between 1918 and 1989 was, we might say, the age of ideology, its vehicle of meaning propaganda, and culture the driver of the vehicle. This is culture as a purported vision of the good society, but concentrated into the expressive and performing arts as transformed by industrial reproduction (film, posters, radio). Mussolini, coming to power in 1921, former socialist editor of the populist newspaper *Avanti!*, and keenly aware of the Communist strongholds in Turin and the north (all supported by Moscow with agitators and funding) offered an ideology with spectacular cultural effects to rival communism.

From this moment onwards, Schiller's and Arnold's conception of culture as the highest as well as the most playful expression of the human mind, 'the best that has been known and thought', is grafted onto a much more spectacular, dramatic, simplified, and above all popular version of the same thing. Arnoldians and Schillerians deprecated this new version of things as vulgar and philistine, which it often was and is. The mighty engineers of capital see this new creature as something they can use for strictly commercial purposes, inventing Hollywood to do the job. Each party, alongside Mussolini and Trotsky, feels the extraordinary force of this new kind of sentimental, simplifying, ideologizing culture.

These are the first clashes of the three titanic ideologies of the twentieth century, Communism, Fascism and Social Democracy or Liberalism – ownership of these last two terms remaining for the whole period much disputed on both sides of the Atlantic. For in truth, the disputes were to prove endemic and epidemic: they killed – say – 70 million people in the epoch which spans the armistice of November 1918 to the collapse of the Soviet empire in 1989. And the competition of the ideologies was first declared on the battleground of culture. The ignorant armies who then fought it out sometimes comprised nations, and sometimes social classes, and sometimes each in bitter contestation with the other.

This radical development can be most economically studied in the two thrilling films commissioned from the state film-director, Leni Riefenstahl, by Hitler and his propaganda minister, Dr Goebbels. *Triumph of the Will* and *Olympic Games 1936* (about the games held in Berlin) both testify to this collusion of culture and political propaganda. The anti-Fascist and Jewish-German social critic of the 1930s, Walter Benjamin, caught this same tendency in a neat aphorism, when he said that 'Fascism aestheticised politics, and Marxism politicised aesthetics'.[9] But in fact the two ideologies and their cultural expression cannot be quite so neatly counterposed. Both made spectacular kitsch (which is to say, grossly sentimentalized and idealized expression) out of the brutal beauty of armaments and military parade; both isolated the leader on high stages for the worship of the people; both celebrated this consummation, and the historical rewriting of nation and party which this required, on film. The key difference was ideological and interpretative: the politics of Soviet art demanded that the proletariat saw their own political experience symbolized in the details of culture; the aesthetics of Fascist art subordinated the *Volk* to the collective mystery of the national leader. For the Bolshevik revolution, Eisenstein made his brilliantly direct cinematic parable, *Battleship Potemkin*. *Olympic Games 1936*, on the other hand, transfigures the effort and rivalry of the games into a balletic hymn to Aryan Fascism (all the lissom, muscled boys and girls are golden haired: only the beautiful black American sprinter, Jesse Owens, darkens the screen). Sport, and the manifold, spontaneous beauty of its innocent ceremonies, not only endorses but reveres the politics which make it happen.

III

These overwhelming, orchestrated spectacles dissolve, at least from this distance, any confident distinction between high and popular culture, although these distinctions will be made for many years yet. They bring out the interpenetration of culture and politics in many ways. First, they show us that mass productive societies have a mass productive leisure as well as politics: *crowds* go to watch the sports, far more than play them; crowds go to watch the great shows of power, tanks, troops, leaders; crowds break production records on behalf of the collective expressions of their will, as sports, soldiers marching, the passion of nations. Secondly, the spectacles indicate the reciprocity of fame and nonentity: the anonymous crowds bestow power on the name of the leader, his name is mighty only in virtue of their recognition. Thirdly, the unprecedented spectacle tells an old story about the nation's continuity, invents a past to support a future, situates the throngs of the people in the new and old roles they must inhabit to make sense of life, and gives them the catchwords they need in order to march to their destiny.

This provision of narratives to live within and purposes to live for *is* culture, and we shall repeat and explore this definition. Here, however, we are practising an as-yet-unnamed but human science – and, as with any science, its scientists must present explanatory theories. Whatever else it may do, cultural theory purports to make the world a little more intelligible, catch hold of the reasons things are as they are, and thereby turn its headlong rush through history a little towards the cause of reason itself.

'Culture' as a term with which to enclose the public displays of Fascism and Communism in the 1930s offers no theory of itself. Indeed, we may suggest once more that, of its nature, culture can hardly lead to self-reflection on the part of a people. There must be some distance between an individual and the culture in which the individual lives and breathes, before life itself can be appraised or analysed.

The bridge over such a gap is built by theory. No doubt some bridges lead somewhere – into the future or into the past – and some do not. But the content of culture, as opposed to the form of politics, cannot generate its own theory. I have already suggested that one definition of culture is that cultures symbolize narratives of how to live – but they cannot provide a critical theory of themselves. The writer, Jenny Turner, once remarked that if you leave a couple of black bags full of rubbish on a street corner, in a few days you will have half a tip there. She went on, 'Culture gathers for no more mysterious reason, but it needs low rents, short leases, slack licensing laws to be able to gather at all'.[10]

Theory, on the other hand, has a sternly tidying-up cast of mind. Its point is to put in order the messiness of cultural life, and to explain to culture the meaning of its outward expressions. Theory and its explanations lend themselves therefore to the forces of legislation and control, never more so than in the case of that sprawling, disorderly, wild and intoxicating creature, the culture.

The pedagogical discourses on culture as propounded by Matthew Arnold and his associates do not deal much in culture of this raucous and sweaty kind. It takes, as we shall see, the anthropologists' reports to add the noise and garishness of culture to its sweetness and light. Culture as way of life, and all that such a term must convey of the imaginative expressiveness of everyday life as well as the great books and works of art, is a vast, protean thing. As the examples of Fascist Italy and Nazi Germany indicate, whatever the political promises, culture may lead to the gates of hell just as well as to the celestial city.

This aspect was first fully confronted by a Communist in Mussolini's Italy. Antonio Gramsci is our first political theorist of culture. Brought up in desperate poverty in Sardinia, while his father was in prison for minor embezzlement, he was sentenced to a hunchback's life by the impacted growth of his torso and shoulders. Throughout his crippled body he felt all the force of a native culture whose enormous weight stultified and subordinated all those classes of people excluded from the exercise of political power and from possession of the culture which supported it.

His name for this monster was 'the hegemony'. Marxism had taught him the ferocious plausibility of a theory of history the driving force of which was the struggle of social classes over the unequal distribution of capital and the fabulous powers it conferred. Marxism, we can readily say, was the first theory of history[11] grounded in the facts of human conflict. It provided, with dazzling clarity and immediate applicability, an explanation of social hatreds and cruelty, together with an inspiring remedy. Trotsky, writing at what seemed to be the gateway to the universal Communist society, had seized with a sure grasp upon how to use the spoils of victory in the forging of a new culture. The past lay open to his pitiless imagination like a tray of surgical utensils.

Gramsci's position, however, was much harder. Unlike the venal and incompetent Romanov government in Russia, estranged from both church and state, the Italian ruling class had at its disposal centuries of Catholicism and of Catholic education. It was suffused by the radiance of Italian art; it had attained an advanced stage of industrialization and had therefore trained a developed class of technicians; and, finally, it had brought to birth (this being crucial to Gramsci's theory of culture-in-politics) a well-established intellectual class loyal to the Italian kingdom then only sixty years old.

Not for Gramsci therefore Trotsky's militant rhetoric. Marxism fired him with its thrilling condensation of thought and action in a philosophy of what Marxists called 'praxis': the fusion of political principle, passionate engagement, and willed purpose in a programme of (preferably revolutionary) reform. He had to hand the first theory in history of 'history as economic struggle' ('dialectical materialism' in the jargon); he added to it the crucial, half-comprehended and limitlessly adaptable ingredient of culture. Where Marx and Engels had seen, for sure, that ruling-class ideas ruled, they had relegated their importance to a position far below the brutal energies of capitalist production. Gramsci corrected this crude dynamic and, in doing so, placed culture itself – ubiquitous, tangible, ungeneralizable – as the ground upon which the figures of politics fight their wars of class.

As far as he was concerned, culture was synonymous with education – education defined as the production, circulation and transmission of both formal and customary knowledge. Intent upon the application of theory not to all human affairs but to Italy, he at once understood – clever, crippled, child of dreadfully poor but not-peasant parents – that a subversive account of culture-as-education must grapple early with the omnipotent form of national instruction canonized by Holy Mother Church and formalized by her partner, the State, now under Mussolini's pious direction.

Mussolini had appointed the celebrated philosopher, Giovanni Gentile, Minister of Education, and Gentile had set in motion certain liberal reforms in opposition to what he and his great intellectual mentor, Benedetto Croce, had stigmatized as the narrow and sterile habits of mere instruction which dominated the church-and-state schools of the day. Gramsci took from Croce the pivotal role which Croce assigned to the intelligentsia in the critique of culture-as-education, but he also prized – a prize personally earned – the painfulness of scholarly labour alongside the respect owed to traditional, even obfuscatory peasant thought, its common-sensible folklore and its zest for magical explanation.

When, in 1927, Mussolini closed down Gramsci's left-wing newspaper and dispatched its leading journalist to prison for the rest of his short life, his prisoner set himself to rewrite the terms of Italian education and, in doing so, to theorize a possible revolution in its culture. Culture in his argument acts its old, idealizing, emancipatory role. For him, certainly, the 'formative capacity ... of a humanistic programme of general culture ... was to a great extent based on the traditionally unquestioned prestige of a particular form of civilisation',[12] but he was absolutely clear that the same old humanism should remain an integral part of a new democratic education. Its plain purpose would be 'to insert young men and women into social activity after bringing them to a certain level of maturity, of capacity for intellectual and practical creativity, and of autonomy of orientation and initiative'. Thus equipped, the same young men and women would be shaped and given purpose by the divisions of intellectual and productive labour as these are ordered by the necessities of modern science and its industrial technology. Parallel to this process, but away to one side, modern society would also produce Gramsci's key political sub-class, the class of the universalizing intellectual, whose product is *writing*.

In enumerating the ideals of ideal culture with such serenity, Gramsci paid his tribute to the necessities of that customary knowledge which lives and thrives in the domestic culture of everyday rules of thumb and precepts of rational thought. He was clear as to the necessity of 'common sense' and of folkloristic habits of explanation and descriptions of causes, and saw them as inhabiting a complementary rather than oppositional place in the building of a popular science.

> Common sense is not a single unique conception, identical in time and space. It is the 'folklore' of philosophy and, like folklore, it takes countless different forms. Its most fundamental characteristic is that it is a conception which, even in the brain of one individual, is fragmentary, incoherent and inconsequential, in conformity with the social and cultural position of those masses whose philosophy it is.[13]

Common sense is, by this token, that everyday culture of feeling and cognition without which new thought has nowhere to grow and nothing upon which to nourish itself. This is one of Gramsci's key theoretic and pedagogic points. Such common sense 'is not something rigid and immobile but is continually transforming itself, enriching itself with scientific ideals and with philosophical opinions which have entered ordinary life'.[14] These are the precipitations and sedimentations of what we are thinking of when we talk about culture as a way of life, and Gramsci stood four-square on the main road of customary usage when he put common-sensible culture at the service of idealizing culture.

He did so, moreover, with a fine flourish which can only rouse the blood of anyone for whom culture retains its power as a call to human solidarity and self-improvement rather than as the all-capacious category in which to throw everything and anything which may glow a little with meaning. One is always struck, reading Gramsci, by his plainness and good sense, the directness of his address to the everyday lives of his comrades, his decency and refusal to touch some of the filthier evasions of communism-in-power, the prospect he holds out for escape from the miseries of Italian poverty if only both the working and the middle classes would rediscover the noble fraternity of Risorgimento.

It is all the more worth recalling these aspects of Gramsci, as well as his simple heroism, since he kept at such work in prison and at a bare table, ill and ill fed, watching every word as he steered it past the prison censor. 'The biography of a man whose business is thinking should be the story of his thought,' wrote R. G. Collingwood, but the story of any thinker is also the story of the circumstances in which the thinking was done, which shaped the thought and framed the feelings inseparable from it. Moreover, thought about culture continues to be of use to us only insofar as it remains charged with particularity.

Gramsci was strong on actuality, and on bending the facts to the cause of usefulness – usefulness in the cause of (first) Italian and (then) human freedom and fulfilment. So when (backed by Moscow roubles) he tackled the circumstances of the Italian working class in the aftermath of the Russian comrades' apparently successful revolution, he was at pains to show how different were the historical contexts and opportunities of Russian as opposed to Italian or any other Western revolutionaries.

Much struck by the analogy of war between classes which was one of Communism's earliest slogans, Gramsci applied the analogy with unusual thoroughness to politics. He saw class warfare as a 'war of position' like the First World War, in which the trenches were the deeply embedded front line of a massive structure of provision and reinforcement. The trenches may be broken into here and there, but unless the vast structure is riddled from below and shifted backwards, such victories are merely tactical. In a famous formulation, 'the superstructures of civil society are like the trench-systems of modern warfare'.[15] For the Italians there could be no sudden coup like Lenin's in 1917, when the Bolsheviks seized power in a country drifting without direction after military defeat. Gramsci taught a tactical trench warfare fought over the class terrain of culture, in which, as in Flanders in 1916, insurgent patrols would go out after dark to search out and to sap the strength of the enemy, his dispositions, lines of command and communication, the quality of his troops, the depth and settlement of his hegemony. The enemy was the enemy because of his power over us and his irresistible encroachment upon our territory. He was, and is, the enemy because he dominated. The issue was (and remains) freedom, and therefore fulfilment, happiness, creation and recreation.

Hegemony has become one of the most-used concepts in the lexicon of cultural enquiry. For Gramsci it had several meanings, mostly derived from the key position the concept occupied in the handbooks of revolution, but directed by him towards understanding the peculiarly specific gravity of bourgeois rule in this century. 'Hegemony' was the name he gave to the successful saturation of an entire society's consciousness by a view of life which suited the bourgeoisie and kept its ruling representatives in power. It was the complex interlocking of cultural institutions – above all, education and schooling, and then the means and instruments of all public communication (books, newspapers, broadcasting) – which won the wholehearted consent of the people to the way things were. Hegemony is counterposed to coercion: its victory is assented to, not compelled. Its realm is 'civil society'; the realm of coercion, on the other hand, is the realm of the state, with its huge advantage in means of violence.

The boundaries between state and 'civil society' are always shifting and never easy to see. Politics, we have suggested, is a figure drawn on the ground of culture; civil society – that uncertain realm of, among other things, public opinion-formation, voluntary association, informal movements, street argument and demonstration, individual rights themselves – is as much cultural as political. It is the zone in which we reconcile the claims of citizenship and the appeal of private pleasures. But however we map the one onto the other, the study of what Gramsci called the hegemony was for him, and remains for us, the study of the question why so many people assent to, and vote for, political arrangements which palpably work against their own happiness and sense of justice. What is it, in schools or on television, which makes rational people accept unemployment, killing queues in hospitals, ludicrous waste on needless weaponry, and all the other awful details of life under modern capitalism? Is the chance of sunny holidays, sexy videos and a modest pay rise per year sufficient answer? This is a problem of hegemony.

Expressed in this way, it is a crude problem, and was even cruder for Gramsci in 1926. But it remains the fundamental problem for us as well. For as long as students of the human sciences in general, and of culture in particular, aspire not only to understand the world as it is but also to imagine it as it ought to be, so they must criticize the one in terms of the other. Where culture (or 'Culture') falls into the sentimentality of kitsch or the cruelty of barbarism, as it does around us every day, then the problem to be explained is the force of hegemony which causes this to happen.

The explicator whom Gramsci appointed for this task was his so-called 'organic intellectual', a sort of popular teacher-journalist who would instruct the proletariat on how to reconcile class passion and peasant commonsense with the weapon of theory and the energy of political organization. The thing to be explained was hegemony, and to do so the people would have to be educated.[16] Gramsci spoke with clear certitude about the necessity of teaching traditional culture to the masses so that that culture becomes their own. Trotsky, as we saw, said much the same thing at the same time, while in England, also in the aftermath of war, a sedately radical Royal Commission on the teaching of English in school, chaired by the high Victorian patriot-poet, Sir Henry Newbolt, came to the selfsame conclusion.[17]

Gramsci was, of necessity, pulled between rhetoric and reason, manifesto appeals and critical analysis. It now looks pretty doubtful as to whether his 'organic intellectual' ever had much chance of being incarnated in a social role, or not at least within the punitive surveillance structures devised by Marxism once it was in power in order to ensure that its leaders continued to lead. Gramsci's advice to do our feeling and thinking at one and the same time (always supposing one could ever do anything else), if we are to be of any use in advancing a historical mission, is no doubt perennially relevant. Such homilies remain at the level of patriotic poetry. Rather, it is in his notes on education[18] that Gramsci provides us with his best example of what it is to study culture and to do so in its essential form, which is symbolic.

Gramsci's example is straightforwardly curricular: he commends Latin literature to an Italian child. On the way, he asks, characteristically: 'would a scholar at the age of 40 be able to sit for 16 hours on end at his worktable if he had not, as a child, compulsorily, through mechanical coercion, acquired the appropriate psycho-physical habits?' Culture, it seems, is no effortless or unconscious process.

In such study, the history of a language is apprehended as its grammar, 'photographed in one abstract moment'. Study of the grammar, nonetheless, brings home forcefully the stylistic differences of different moments in its constitution; the student acquires a semantics but lives a history. Nor does she study Latin to learn a language but, rather, to capture a myth and let it roam her imagination. Thus she enters her 'whole cultural tradition, which also and particularly lives outside the school'.[19]

IV

Politics, that 'noble art', was to have been the redemptive method of the nineteenth century. The great patriarchs of such thought – Mill, William Morris and Marx, de Tocqueville and Alexander Herzen, Emerson and T. H. Green – counted on politics to bring the idea of a common good to public recognition. In the twentieth century, such a vision of politics was swallowed up in the vastnesses of culture. Gramsci had tried to politicize his comrades in a cultural struggle; Trotsky had merely assumed that politics could fashion culture to its own purposes; the much more terrible and inclusive politics of German Fascism, however, showed its opponents that once culture saturates politics with its all-pervasiveness, its novel power to soak into the stuff of personal identity, this makes culture – impossible of abstract definition as it is – a monster of the deepest meanings a society may have, and a creature capable of infinite destruction.

It is at the hands of the two great German social critics, Theodor Adorno and Max Horkheimer, that culture takes on its darkest hue.

It is invidious to take these two master-theorists in isolation from their colleagues. They met at the extraordinary Frankfurt Institute for Social Research, a private centre for public thinking paid for by radical millionaire Felix Weil, which opened in a specially designed, stylishly modernist building in June 1924.[20] The (invited) members of the Institute had no students and their only commitment was to publish their thoughts on the state of the world.

They were cast as intellectuals in opposition from the outset, a role enhanced by the fact that most members came from Jewish families. An explicit interest of its research programme was the strong vein of anti-Semitism in German society. When anti-Semitism burst into the main arteries of government and power, the Institute was swept into exile, first to Geneva, then to New York. Long before its departure, however, it had diagnosed the hideousness and terror of which modern popular movements regulated by impersonally modern bureaucracies would prove capable. These men were hardly examples of Gramsci's 'organic' intellectuals, but the nature of their work and its context, as the Weimar republic failed and the Nazis rose to power, were sufficient to sustain the intellectual ardour of Adorno and Horkheimer and their remarkable fellows.

Almost all of them had been reared to admire and delight in the traditional account of culture as best embodied in the best of art, none more so than Adorno. He was taught music by the great early modern composer Berg, became a friend and associate of Berg's rival Schoenberg, and was no mean pianist himself. But all of the Institute's members concluded that the old culture had been irrevocably displaced from high office, and came to view what replaced it, whether in Hitler's Germany or post-war America, as no less irrevocably poisoned by populism and cheapened by commercialism.

From its foundation, the Institute assumed a deliberately Marxist cast of thought. From its Jewishness and the sacred books of the Talmud, it borrowed, first, its characteristic idiom – a strong taste for paradox, a keen eye for enigma, and sheer difficulty – a judicious pessimism, secondly, and (particularly the Viennese Adorno) its loyalty to Freud. All its members were naturally and profoundly Hegelian and Kantian by way of their education in German philosophy.

Their concern was to unite the idealism of the two first German masters with the 'dialectical materialism' of Marx and the clinical theorizing of that hitherto undiscovered area of the mind, the subconscious, brought to light by Freud. The result would be an emancipatory method for a science of human affairs adequate to the twentieth century.

This was Critical Theory (the Frankfurters' capital letters), and it was peculiarly suited to theorizing and criticizing the dense social totality and its unprecedented forms under the heading of culture. The theory was well matched to the task, enormous though it was. But the task itself, urgent as Adorno and Horkheimer felt it to be, also aroused their intense distaste. They were passionately committed to the optimism inscribed on the banners of socialism, and grimly convinced that socialism had no chance of fulfilment. The hysteria of Fascism in Germany destroyed all hope for a rationally just and equal society. The corrosions of American individualism joined to the garish success of American capitalism similarly cancelled out what Adorno saw as 'the promise of happiness' held out by high art, but only so long as it was immunized by seriousness and truthfulness against the madness of money and the intoxication of kitsch.

When they had finished, they hoped to have dissolved the old distinction between idealism and materialism (the belief that the world is made up by our ideas about it as opposed to the belief that it is made what it is by external facts, especially economic ones). Thereby they would overcome the bloody old dualisms which so disfigured Western philosophy and the failed effort to devise an emancipatory human science. Body vs mind, reason vs passion, individual vs society, objective vs subjective, had all rendered a truly human science either impotent or antagonistic. Such oppositions had made criticism in terms of 'the best which has been known and thought' impossible. Hence, society had no external measure of human betterment. Critical Theory would interpret the promise of happiness held out and implied in all cultural expression, and use that interpretation to evaluate what that culture did in keeping the promise.

When these stern, ascetic men came to it, they made a bleak report. They were faced, first, with locating culture, as subject and object of enquiry. In a capitalist society, utterly unprecedented in its transformation of all values into prices, culture is encircled by commerce. As far as the Frankfurters were concerned this was as true of American culture in the late 1940s as of German culture in the 1930s. The amazing plenitude of America nonetheless filled a totalitarian society. Freedom to choose, as it is now a cliché to say, was only freedom obediently to choose a different consumer commodity.

The critical theorists of Frankfurt wanted an empirically verifiable theory of society. They wanted to discern the general lines of historical development, but to keep faith with subjective peculiarities and resistance to general trends. They wanted to accommodate a full recognition of the contradictoriness of things within the large totality of historical epochs and transitions. And they wanted a picture of a society in which reason and happiness could be imagined in harmony, a picture which in their view was daily defiled by both capitalism and Fascism, but which same picture was kept alive by a decently democratic view of great art.

It was, and is, a lot to want; especially for Marxists who not only saw that totalitarianism impended in Europe, but who also became increasingly incredulous about the liberating role assigned by the prophetic arm of Marxism to the working class. They were, they came to conclude, studying a historical process with no subjects in it. The old plot, with its heroic proletariat and villainous bourgeoisie, could no longer be believed. By the time the Institute went into exile and Hitler came to power, there was no political party which its members could join, the visions of revolution were discredited by Communism and Fascism, and the people as the vanguard of emancipation had conspicuously disgraced themselves in the Third Reich.

As a result, the Institute had to re-create everything from scratch: a theory to explain what had gone wrong with politics and culture, and the one because of the other; a plausible hopefulness and a collective subject (a party, say, or a nation) capable of turning hope into action; an intellectual method flexible, bold and sensitive enough to uphold universals but to resist tyranny. The venture failed, as all its labourers agreed. The task for us is to decide whether the journey without any arrival is enough for us to admire and emulate in the different (but prophesied) polity of present consumerism, with specific reference to Adorno's and Horkheimer's joint classic, *The Dialectic of the Enlightenment*.[21] This weird but magnificent book serves to remind us of the heavy connections which join the way we enquire into the world, criticizing what we find, to absolute presuppositions about the way the world is and the intellectual genealogy which made those presuppositions what they are.

The two men begin with a strange re-reading of Homer's Odysseus myth by way of establishing something archetypal in the passage of individual identity out of prehistory. 'It is homesickness,' they write in a characteristic paradox, 'that gives rise to the adventures through which subjectivity (whose fundamental history is presented in the *Odyssey*) escapes from the prehistoric world'. Thus our authors provide themselves with a schematic little fable of human emancipation, in which the self, forever called to by the lost homeland, makes itself an identity on the journey back. Returning home is at once a restoration and an imprisonment.

Each of Odysseus's adventures on the long journey teaches the shaping, self-interpreting identity to win freedom by virtue of self-discipline, renunciation, and refusal of the 'oceanic bliss', in Freud's phrase, of prehistoric, infantile union with nature. This is never more true than in the famous episode with the sirens, when Odysseus, determined to hear their ravishing music but knowing that he will give way to their blandishments if he can and thereby doom both his crew and himself to drowning, stops the mariners' ears with wax and has himself bound to the mast. Thus the crew cannot hear his orders to change course towards the sirens, while Odysseus can listen to the music but do nothing about it. So the self forcibly denies its childish longings while adoring them for what they are. The self chastens itself in order to become itself; this is a psychic rhythm. After the Enlightenment, say our two cultural theorists, it takes on a psychotic circularity. Psychosis designates a rhythm of compulsion and gratification of a regular but unregulable kind, in which the play of fantasy upon experience is such as to preclude rational reflection or the direction of action towards diverse ends. The only cure is recognition of the cycle. When the repressed narrative is reclaimed by the clinician (in our case, the clinician as cultural historian), it may be given to the patient for incorporation into a new and liberated narrative of the future.

Adorno and Horkheimer interpret Homer in such a way as to bring out the mutilation of reason incipient in all historical development. With the Enlightenment, they say, that incipient menace rises to the rim of the epoch and overflows. The principle of reason is exalted above history, custom and experience; reason is set to determine the facts by objective observation, and to dominate the outer processes of the natural world as well as the inner processes of human nature by the will to power.

It is this process which has become psychotic in the modern world, and from which Adorno and Horkheimer see very little chance of escape. Reason has been demoralized; it has no intrinsic relation to morality, law, or science. Art, classically the home of a passionate striving for transcendence, has been coarsened and sweetened by the cultural industries until it has passed almost incurably into the narcotic and saccharine cartoons of kitsch. Even the avant-garde, once the shocking gypsy-cousin of the bourgeoisie, has been paid off as designer of the next fashion but one.

The agent of this deadly process is what Max Weber named *Zweckrationalität*, which translates clumsily as 'goal-rationality'. I shall call it technicism. Technicism has captured reason, and stripped it of the ethical aura with which in the classical field of vision it was compounded. Reason is now a strictly formal process without any of its previous links to virtue, moderation or justice. It simply reports on the most efficient means to a given end (*Zweck*). The insatiable demands of capitalism for effective production in order to saturate every market at the appropriately measured level of satisfaction turn *praxis* (craft) and *poesis* (art) into technique. Technique is bereft of human agency. Technique may be taught as a disembodied process; it is best done by machines and supervised by technicians. Each technician must be readily substitutable, all his operations routinized. Thus judgement, apprenticeship, experience, mastery, art, and craft which, taken together, constitute the customs of culture, are all eradicated. Technical reason, controlling technology, has reduced the beautiful world of making and thinking, creating and criticizing, to the flowchart.

This is a paraphrase of Adorno's deathly vision, and the fulcrum chapter of *The Dialectic of the Enlightenment* is the structural analysis which its author makes (this was Adorno's work alone) of the so-called 'cultural industries'. This latter term is one of his key polemical coinages, even though it has now entirely lost its derogatory edge. For Adorno, the sumptuous culture of *fin de siècle* Vienna and Berlin, which was for both of them a touchstone of value, had been pervaded and putrefied by the absoluteness of capital. Culture in those capitals meant what it meant to Arnold and Sainte-Beuve, Ruskin and Schiller: it meant the noblest new architecture, the most experimental and startling new music, the irresistible fascination of all that was most difficult in contemporary poetry and painting, the significance for the common good given to that recalcitrant and motley crowd of marginal journeymen-artists, the avant-garde. But Adorno and his colleague saw piercingly how culture, purportedly the domain of universal or transcendental value, had been degraded by capitalism into something to be sold for a profit like everything else. It was an analysis which sorted easily with what we shall find specifically literary commentators saying about consumer culture in England at the same time, with the striking difference that for Adorno and Horkheimer the culprit was specifically capitalism, and with the added force that Freudian psychoanalysis gave to a politics derived from Marx but modified by their own scepticism and prescience.

It is important to ward off those many simpletons who say, more or less, that the Frankfurters were a bunch of stuck-up intellectuals brought up on Viennese and Berlin culture at its most rarefied, and who would be incapable of unaffected enjoyment in any case. Adorno, like all his colleagues, kept open a wide space in his good society for happiness, and even the pitiful and spirit-sugaring happiness created by the most syrupy Hollywood romance 'participates in the truth-content of happiness . . . no individual happiness is possible which does not virtually imply that of society as a whole'.[22] Adorno fervently hoped for 'the promise of happiness' held out by all art, to be kept to a whole people. What he saw was that its present fulfilment by the cultural industries was a paltry deceit:

The culture industry perpetually cheats its consumers of what it perpetually promises. The promissory note which, with its plots and staging, it draws on pleasure is endlessly prolonged; the promise, which is actually all the spectacle consists of, is illusory: all it actually confirms is that the real point will never be reached . . . The secret of aesthetic sublimation is its representation of fulfilment as a broken promise. The culture industry does not sublimate; it represents. By repeatedly exposing the objects of desire, breasts in a clinging sweater or the naked torso of the athlete hero, it only stimulates the unsublimated forepleasure which habitual deprivation has long since reduced to a masochistic semblance. There is no erotic situation which, while insinuating and exciting, does not fail to indicate unmistakably that things can never go that far . . . Works of art are ascetic and unashamed; the culture industry is pornographic and prudish. Love is downgraded to romance . . . The mass production of the sexual automatically achieves its repression.[23]

This is the cultural corner of the perfectly technological society. Such a society is already totalitarian: 'A technological rationale is the rationale of domination itself. It is the coercive nature of society alienated from itself. Automobiles, bombs and movies keep the whole thing together.' If there is a sloganeering element in these aphorisms, this is because of the totalizing sweep of an argument which takes in animated cartoons, private sexual lives, car design, and the spectacle of political authority as rendered in the newsreels, each a part of universally technologized experience.

This is the system which ensures that every consumer will feel to the bottom of their heart the unfulfillable yearning to carry on consuming. Such a society will reproduce itself more or less exactly. The possibility of its discovering in its forms the outline of the better society which is its negative or transcendent image becomes less and less feasible. The only conclusion for the intellectual is pessimism; Adorno reached his conclusion before the end of the Second World War, for all that he continued to write prolifically until his death in 1969.

Adorno's controlled distaste for a culture suffused with the values of consumer capitalism sounds consistently through his mordant and ironic prose. Such a culture, he contends, will lose the capacity to be serious about itself, to find out what it is worth to itself, in a currency that cannot be converted into investment values. Nonetheless, he still catches hold of that vivid promise of happiness which gleams on the other side of Marxism, and shines out from his few flashes of sympathetic pleasure.

For Adorno, the location of this possibility and the (transient) fulfilment of the promise was art. Mozart always rouses him to this reaffirmation:

> As radiant things give up their magic claims [Adorno is talking about *The Magic Flute*], renounce the power with which the subject invested them and hoped with their help himself to wield, they become transformed into images of gentleness, promises of a happiness cured of domination over nature. This is the primeval history of luxury, that has migrated into the meaning of all art.[24]

As he goes on to say, it is capitalism which crassly insists on the question, 'What for?', and insists on it with regard to art, when it is the *point* of art that it negates that very question. The trouble is that 'the closer the mode of production of artefacts comes to material mass production, the more naively the question is provoked'. Even the very best television programmes today are realizations of Adorno's bleak prophecy.

Only works of art silence the questions, 'What for?' and 'How much?'. Adorno not only respects but gives his heart to the happiness capitalism makes possible, and he gives his head to the prevention of art turning into kitsch. Kitsch is the killer according to the Frankfurt critique of the modern cultural industries. Kitsch is the inevitable product of all totalitarianisms, whether Fascism, Stalinism, or the blank and enveloping totalitarianisms of the shopping mall. Kitsch removes the truth from art, and substitutes consolation; it tells us, sweetly, that *everything will be all right*.

For Adorno and his colleagues, capitalist culture serves only the impersonal drive of capital to turn that *everything* into an adjunct of the economy. If culture makes the place where we live and politics teaches how to live, kitsch consumerism is the narcotic which suppresses the mighty question of how to live well; instead, it turns the home of our culture into an unacknowledged prison for the gratification of trivial desires. Thus culture brims over and dowses the flames of politics and its morality. It becomes egregious.

By a strange twist, it is helped in this hubris by anthropology, the twentieth-century science of culture, which seized upon the name of science so confidently that it was able to dismiss the art of politics from its purview for a whole generation.

3
Culture and the Science of Humanity

I

When, in 1871, the true begetter of anthropology as a discipline, Sir Edward Tylor, published *Primitive Culture* at the age of thirty-nine, he not only formalized that usage of culture as identifying a distinct and distant way of life, he also ratified the study of exotic peoples as a way of criticizing the folks at home. Nor was that all. *Primitive Culture* and Tylor's predecessor volume, *Researches into the Early History of Mankind* (1865), mark the decisive moment in British intellectual history at which the systematic study of social institutions begins. At the same time, Tylor and J. S. Mill joined in the determined attempt to bring to all such study the dual focus of antidote to egoism and arrogance, provided by careful comparison with the way other societies do things.

The repellent propensity of Victorian England to congratulate itself on the unique good fortune of being English was famously satirized by Dickens in *Our Mutual Friend* and in the figure of Mr Podsnap.

> 'We Englishmen are Very Proud of our Constitution, Sir,' Mr Podsnap explained with a sense of meritorious proprietorship, 'It was Bestowed upon us By Providence. No other country is so Favoured as this Country . . .' 'And *other* countries,' said

the foreign gentleman, 'They do how?' 'They do, Sir,' returned
Mr Podsnap, gravely shaking his head, 'they do – I am sorry
to be obliged to say it – as they do.'

This offensive spirit may still be sniffed in those various
middle-aged corners of British and American society where
the *Daily Mail* and the *New York Post* are substituted for
more self-aware reading matter, and it was for Tylor and such
distinguished allies as Sir James Frazer (as it was at the same
time for that spokesman of the intelligentsia, Matthew
Arnold) a prime polemical commitment to put down
Podsnappery.

Tylor, Frazer and, a little later, the giant of the new field,
Émile Durkheim, were, as a straightforward consequence of
ethnographic method, committed to confirming just how
humanly various being a human being was. They were fired
by the ideal of making a science of society out of the discipline of empirical observation as taught by their Enlightenment forebears, but the observable facts did much to mitigate
Enlightenment optimism. From its beginning, social anthropology cherished Herder's maxims and Rousseau's sym-
pathies; the anthropologists found and taught the variety of
experience, whether the experience of religion, of kinship and
of courting, of sexual custom and all the imbrications of
marriage, or of the rules and roles of trade and exchange –
all these and much more gathered under the heading of
culture.

By Tylor's and Frazer's day, they all did so in the shadow
of the towering achievement of Charles Darwin. As anthropology compiled its founding narrative, it was bound to predi-
cate all human development as evolutionary, and the advent
of science as a mark of progress. Darwin's discoveries had of
course dealt a fatal blow to fundamentalist Christianity; the
book of Genesis was shown to be a myth, Adam's ancestry
was replaced by that of the higher primates, and simian creatures turned out to be longer lived and more adaptable than
human beings. Frazer, acolyte of historical science not religion, made clear to thousands of readers of his best-selling
classic, *The Golden Bough* (1898), just how local a folktale
the myth of the Jewish Son of God was, as well as how
widespread the alternative tales of divine resurrection. Tylor,

though relishing the jolt to respectable English middle-class believers administered by the tall tales of anthropology, was as intent, he believed, upon a true life science as were the busy lepidopterists, geologists, entomologists and (come to that) etymologists and psychologists of the day. He was classifying cultures just as they were classifying arachnids, geostratification periods, butterflies, semantics, hysterics, and lianas.

Culture was for Tylor an unproblematic term. It connoted custom, folklore, ceremony, belief and ritual, rather than social structure, all conceived as rooted in the pre-industrial community of implicit solidarities, shared labour and common beliefs.[1] Tylor worked in and on these exotic home-linesses, in part because of a naturalistic and evolutionary belief that in simple or primitive societies he would discover the original form from which modern society had developed. On the whole, he ignored Durkheim's rigorous emphasis upon social structure, the powerful preoccupation of the French and the later British anthropological traditions, and, by following a then-very-prevalent set of interests in dreams, prophecy and visions, as well as the folklore of ghosts and spirits – all the beliefs, cults, superstitions and stories clustered at the gates of birth and death – he single-handedly established a large proportion of the subject's content and a working definition of the content of culture itself. After Tylor, no anthropologist could omit either the facts of life or the beliefs they carry with them – 'birth and copulation and death' as T. S. Eliot's crude character Sweeney puts it in 1930 or so ('that's all the facts when you're down to brass tacks').

Tylor, like so many of his contemporaries (and, no doubt, like us), was pulled in two different directions by his subject and his own intellectual formation. His Enlightenment origins, his Darwinian commitment, his allegiance to science and to the unseating of religious irrationality, all led him to study primitive cultures for the sake of progress, and to see emancipation as the dissolution of superstitious animism (this last a term which Tylor gave to anthropology). His tradition of thought anticipated the coming to maturity of modern scepticism, and the victory of its Kantian hero, that judiciously rational, freely choosing and confidently intentional character who provides the contemporary ideal of mature adulthood.[2]

Culture for such a figure is the instrument of intelligent action and of well-kept feelings. But culture, for any sensitive anthropologist taught by Tylor and then initiated further into the subject by Tylor's great successors, was an idea that pulled human scientists back into the past as much as it drew them forward into the future. Rousseau's cry of anguish from the previous century – 'man is born free but is everywhere in chains' – was too plainly true of industrial capitalist society for anthropologists to ignore the graceful-looking ease of life and the calm dignity of so many primitive peoples. The Polish-Englishman, Bronislaw Malinowski, once notoriously confessed to himself while in the Trobriand Islands and reading Conrad's *Heart of Darkness*, 'on the whole my feelings toward the natives are decidedly tending to "Exterminate the brutes".'[3] None the less, in his celebrated studies, the very titles of which sing plaintively of Odysseus' homesickness, *The Sexual Life of Savages in Northwestern Melanesia* (1929), *Argonauts of the Western Pacific* (1922), *Coral Gardens and Their Magic* (1935), Malinowski almost involuntarily drew upon and restored that strong charge of longing and wistfulness carried by the concept of culture from the start. When culture connotes a way of life it does so *in contrast* to the external way of life which supplies the context from which the term is being applied. Contrasting, as we noted, is inherent in the anthropological meaning of the word. Given, however, that the subject-matter of anthropology emphasizes from its beginning *primitive* cultures – the concept plural, the adjective exotic – it was impossible then (as it is now) to discard the implicit contrast with the distant way of life as a secret garden. After all, the very etymology of 'paradise' is from the Persian *pairi* meaning 'around' (as in *para*bola) and *douza* meaning 'wall'.[4] Culture, then, is the happily unselfconscious, pre-modern and carefree way of life of a simple people in a secret garden, whom we can observe over the anthropologist's shoulder but cannot join.

II

The tension in the concept of culture between a lost past and an unreachable future was later compounded when the great ancestors of the subject were accused by the briefly radical generation of the 1960s of codifying primitive cultures so that imperial politics could do with them as it wished. The charge of complicity with imperialism was easily generalized across the subject, and the implications of this for discussion of the meaning of a concept as understood in terms of the history of its use are once again contradictory. For the men who really colonized the subject of anthropology in the wake of the first explorers, those quintessential Englishmen (I speak without mockery), Sir Alfred Radcliffe-Brown and his fellow *seigneur* (and junior by a decade), Sir Edward Evan Evans-Pritchard, the study of other cultures was the strictly non-political (because strictly scientific) study of the behaviour of remote peoples.

That those peoples were, sometimes but not always, subjects of the British empire, was of no concern to our two worthies. Radcliffe-Brown and Evans-Pritchard addressed themselves judiciously to the task of understanding and describing other cultures[5] for the sake of a human science, regardless of whether that science would be called to the service of an empire which they both regarded as a more-or-less benign influence in regions of the globe where, in its absence, things might be even bloodier than they were.

The amenability of culture to scientific observation was not in doubt for these second-generation anthropologists, and their classifications confirm the content of the concept for all those later, and professionally non-anthropological, commentators who want to talk about the meanings and values of everyday life. As Evans-Pritchard himself said, in a series of BBC talks in 1951 intended to explain to interested amateurs what the subject was about:[6]

> most of the anthropologists of the last century would have regarded culture and not social relations as the subject-matter of their inquiries; and culture was for them something concrete. They thought of exogamy, tokenism, matriliny,

ancestor worship, slavery and so forth as customs – things – and it was an inquiry into these customs, or things, that they regarded themselves as pursuing. Consequently their concepts had always to carry such a heavy load of cultural reality that comparative analysis was bogged down at the outset.

Evans-Pritchard goes on to commend the comparative study of societies 'on the basis of their social structures rather than of their cultures' and no doubt he had in mind his powerful senior partner in the venture, Radcliffe-Brown, for whom the facts of identification in the matter of structure were as hard and unmistakable as stone. Structures have functions, and given that primitive societies and other cultures can and must be observed as enclosed totalities, the discovery of structure and the identification of its components are at the same time the determination of 'a condition in which all parts of the social system work together with a sufficient degree of harmony or internal consistency to continue as a system, i.e. without producing persistent conflicts which can neither be resolved nor regulated.'[7] Functionalism, in other words, tells the tale that every social practice *functions*, and does so as an essential part in the systematization of society; without each such component the society in question would lapse into persistent and irresolvable conflict.

Functionalism is a powerful and useful explanatory instrument. But it cannot count as a satisfactory theory. It cannot, in the last resort, discriminate between function and dysfunction. Saturnalian revels, for example, when a whole social group goes out on the town for a bit of an orgy, turns the world upside down, mocks the rulers, and blasphemes the priests, may functionally be explained as a necessary letting-off of steam without which caste resentments and inequalities would boil unstoppably over. The trouble with such explanations is that there is no sure way of telling the difference between saturnalia and rowdiness on a large scale and downright political insurrection, with broken windows, drunkenness and brass bands to match. In both cases the police turn up, bash people over the head, and make sure everything is tidied up by Monday morning. Functionalism is inseparable from judgement – judgement as to whether the commotion in question composes or disconcerts the social order. (Industrial strikes may, for an example closer to home, easily go either way).

The sheer usefulness of functionalism and of its sibling, structuralism, cannot be doubted. Both, one might conjecture, derive strength from the moment of their coinage, when the stupendous success of nineteenth-century engineering provided human scientists with such a rich array of metaphors. Bridges, engine-rooms, railways, propellers, had structures, frictions, dynamics and above all energy. Since all metaphors are testable, the anthropologists could treat customs as experiments and, over time, determine how the social machinery drove itself clatteringly forward, held itself together in all its extraordinary parts, found and filled itself with fuel, improved itself, and became more efficient.

It seems likely that such enquiry took as much from practical scientific method as it did from imperial preference for treating primitive, exotic, or native peoples as living in enclosed totalities. Certainly, the classical anthropological fieldworkers of the great tradition cut clean out of their field of vision the soldiers, policemen, administrators, tax collectors, and governor-generals who together ensured that the people in question remained amiably docile and productive. The intellectual contribution of Radcliffe-Brown, Claude Lévi-Strauss, Raymond Firth and company came in any case rather too late to be much use to the last vestiges of old empire, and their sons and heirs – Peter Worsley, Pierre Bourdieu – set themselves on the contrary to subvert what was left of it.

The principle of method which excluded politics and concentrated on culture was largely scientific. The Azande, the Tikopia, the Nambi Kwara, the Trobriand Islanders were, at the time the first ethnographers arrived, pretty well enclosed peoples. Where politics, to the imperial nations, simply *was* the clash of powers, the struggle between classes, and the quarrel over territory, these numerically small, geographically remote, globally indifferent tribes-without-nationhood had no politics; that was precisely what made them exotic and primitive. What they had was what you saw: custom, ritual, religion, ceremony, kinship – 'birth and copulation and death'

– and these elemental constituents provided the thick stuff, the observable *things* of culture. Abstraction – ritual, superstition (in other words, what we do not believe but they do), kinship, and so forth – stood close to actuality. Fertility in Papua was a matter of what people did with seed and semen and song; warding off witchcraft in Java was a busy business of anxious action, marking out ground, paying off and kitting out the spell-binder; coming-of-age among the Nuer was half-a-dozen incisions cut with a small knife from ear to ear and to the depth of the skull bone.

These domestic and excessive commonplaces and *what they mean* are defined, as a matter of craft-practice and the academic divisions of labour, as culture. Etymology and semantics are more than a match for pure science, but then, in the science of human affairs, so is literature. Hence, for all their empirical fidelity, the anthropologists could not rid their key concept of its idealizing connotations, nor lose from it the contrastive implication that culture was and is something precious that is possessed by simpler societies but which has been lost to those who have followed progress, achieved development, and become most unhappily rich.

At the same time, those 'founders of anthropological discursivity',[8] were not so innocent that they believed they were writing down purely scientific knowledge without the intervention of an author. Theirs was authoritative authorship in part because they discovered things new to their readership if not to their subject-matters but, more than that, because they did not only record them, they *created* them, and they did so, as Bishop Sprat recommended, in a 'close, naked, natural way of speaking; positive expression, clear senses; a native easiness',[9] thus, the marks of art upon the signs of science.

III

To speak of the affairs of other human beings is always and necessarily to dramatize them in narrative. Malinowski and Evans-Pritchard, Lévi-Strauss and Ruth Benedict,[10] 'founders of discursivity' every one of them, each spoke in an unmistakably and personally authoritative voice, tone, and manner, almost always with a polemical edge and a rhetorical gleam. They put their names, of course, to the pledge to objectivity, but culture in all its weird and protean manifestations is only there if the observer is, first, sharp and sensitive enough to see, hear, touch, taste, or smell it, and, secondly, only there if he or she can persuade the rest of us that that was what there was. When Ruth Benedict, announcing that she practises 'the science of custom', falls into her account of Kwakiutl Indians of the Pacific sea-coast of Alaska, she joins at the same time the long tradition of travellers' tale-telling, calmly describing what so few people and only one human scientist (not her, as it happens, though she does not say so) have been to see.

> Like most of the American Indians, except those of the South-West pueblos, the tribes of the North-West Coast were Dionysian. In their religious ceremonies the final thing they strove for was ecstasy. The chief dancer, at least at the high point of his performance, should lose normal control of himself and be rapt into another state of existence. He should froth at the mouth, tremble violently and abnormally, do deeds which would be terrible in a normal state. Some dancers were tethered by four ropes held by attendants, so that they might not do irreparable damage in their frenzy. Their dance songs celebrated this madness as a supernatural portent . . . The dancer meanwhile danced with glowing coals held in his hands. He played with them recklessly. Some he put in his mouth, others he threw about among the assembled people, burning them and setting fire to their cedar-bark garments. When the Bear Dancers danced, the chorus sang . . . The Bears were dressed for their great ceremonies completely in black bearskins, and even on lesser occasions they wore upon their arms the skins of the bear's forelegs with all the claws displayed.[11]

It is a gripping passage, incredible and immediate by turns. It swerves back and forth over the sacred line dividing science from art, and does so, of course, in the profane name of culture, dissolving the hardest distinctions. Nonetheless, Benedict and her sister-anthropologist, Margaret Mead, may be taken as the two practitioners of their artistic science who first urged upon their colleagues the plausibility of a reversion of the terms for a season, and of trying out a science of art.

The pair of them were, no doubt, the most famous anthropologists in the world to the 1 million readers who bought their books. Mead had, you might say, single-handedly changed the sexual lives of the cultivated bourgeoisie by her polemically intended, much-disputed, imaginatively irresistible accounts of *Coming of Age in Samoa* and baby-minding in Bali, and she certainly was not one to sacrifice[12] a cracking good yarn to mere scepticism. Nevertheless, the works of the two women may be used as signposts in the schism which divides their generation of the participant-observation of culture from the next one, which broke so decisively with the official canons of social science.

It should be emphasized that this part of the story is not being represented as a victory for the new thinkers over the old in the anthropological battle of the books. Clive James once observed brilliantly that, in television's reconstructive documentaries, the history of science is dramatized as a lot of men with white beards disbelieving one man with a black beard, who is nonetheless proved right. Victory in anthropology is less straightforward. As we have seen, the great ethnographers wrote literature as well as human science; they summoned up their scholarly as well as their class authority in order to be believed; they marked out with unselfquestioning certainty the realms of human conduct which they would study.

They could not help, however, reflecting the 'absolute presuppositions' (R. G. Collingwood's phrase, already encountered) which they had absorbed and with which they had to work – no more than we can, with our historically different ones. Those presuppositions instructed them to test the metaphors of engineering science – structure, framework, function, and the like – in the separable social architecture of other cultures (and because other, distant and circumscribed). Those methods (without which they could not have told their tales nor made their discoveries, nor – as they did – gradually changed the mind of their originary nations) could not, however, survive the recognition brought by world war.

Before the word 'globalization' was coined, the twentieth century discovered that the globe is a single sphere and the peoples on it as indissolubly members one of another as they are incontrovertibly at one another's throats.

In the anthropological beginning, however, and in order to arrive at adequate explanations (such as would obey the severe injunction of William of Occam seven centuries before not to multiply causes but to confine oneself to what is needed in order to explain sufficiently), the founding anthropologists had to cut out of their field of vision everything extraneous to a plain description and a strict explanation. (Hence, no doubt, their concentration on Last Things: death, witchcraft, sex, trade.) So those pioneer men and women obeyed Sir Francis Bacon's precept, they counted and recounted before classifying. They counted up what people did and how many times they did it, and told the tall tale of what they saw and how often they saw it.

As is the way with new forms of thought and of knowledge, the next generation must needs begin with the old forms and language, and then find that they do not fit. By the mid-1980s, it had come to seem to successors from the old and new imperialising nations, that the plain tales from the hills narrated by the old guard were not all they seemed, and that to present them so bluntly as the products of science was both necessary and disingenuous. The customs and ceremonies caught by the *grands seigneurs* of anthropology at the last moment of immutability (the British empire attained its largest expanse in 1932)[13] were being changed utterly by the world of new nations (155 of them since the foundation of the United Nations in 1946), new trade, new roads and refugees, new medicines, new wars cold and hot, and new rumours of worse wars to come.

These larger things had long been creeping up on the Azande, the Trobriand Islanders, and all others who had not been counted into world history, of course, but to see them at all in the first place was to see such peoples as different, cut sharply out and off from the rest of the world. It had been a dictum of Marx and Engels in 1848 that all history was become world history, but it took another century for the scientists of human affairs to believe them and act on the aphorism.

They did so because people were living by it. Culture certainly lives in things, but the use to which the things are put, whether ideas, instruments, or feelings, change when they have to. One way of writing the history of anthropology after 1945 would be to study how culture-as-things changed into culture-as-history, and how the ways of understanding discarded the old lists and the careful recounting, and licensed itself instead to tell stories and histories. Licence may be, well, licentious, but the change corroborated a new and radical unease with things, however solidly countable they remained.

Treating culture as things has this supreme advantage: that such a presupposition enjoins steadiness. Things do not move unless you push them. They were being pushed around by bigger and clumsier fists than anthropologists' by the 1960s. Travel broadens the mind all right, and the anthropologists have long protested their subject be preceded by the adjective 'comparative'. Once the strictly local news was in, from Polynesia, East Africa, the Arctic Tundra, the further reaches of the Amazon, and fieldnotes turned into syllabuses, it was no longer enough to advertise the variety of cultural experience, indispensable as that first step was. Comparisons brought out in protuberant if also blurred relief the fact that varieties may be incomparable, that the constants of sex and shelter, food and death receive universal dues of cultural respect, but paid in so many currencies that abstractions break up into their concrete, local components. Culture itself is then best not defined but pointed at; it is everywhere in domestic life, and everywhere in politics also, once one has the hang of other such dreary abstractions as power and status.

These discoveries (for that is what they were, and their novelty caused one father of the discourse, Claude Lévi-Strauss, to declare the preparation of a periodic table of the elements of culture his life's work) led different anthropologists in different directions, but all of them turning away from what a new pejorative called 'reification' – literally, turning all human action and actors into an agglomeration of objects. To make all things into objects to all men was to make an elementary mistake about human oddity. Objectification had perhaps been necessary in order to start up the human sciences at all, but a redefinition of the subject (and its object) must now lead, as intellectual enquiry through the centuries always has led, to the marking of a fresh boundary between natural and human sciences. The naturalists treated of objects unaffected by observation and moved by causes; the humanists watched subjects that were themselves liable to learn from observational theory, to change conduct in the light of what other people (including theorists) made of it, and in any case moved as much by reasons and their passions as by historical causes.

This courteous and violent argument rolled over the years between 1950 and 2000; and it is not over yet. But the old ambition to make the study of society into a science as hard as engineering or old-fashioned physics has gone, and good riddance. Indeed, it was as much dispelled at the insistence of the elderly hard-heads,[14] who set the necessary but un-meetable conditions for any such human enquiry to count as proper science, as it was by soft-hearted humanists[15] complaining about the dereliction of human solidarity at the hands of the rat-and-pigeon minders.

IV

Changes of mind are never as complete as the anthologies or the textbooks claim. Scientism still has plenty of running in it, and humanists have, in a small way, had their revenge on science. Over forty years ago Thomas Kuhn[16] famously showed just how human – because competitive, inflexible, bound by custom, age, authority – indeed, just how much a matter of *habit* science has proved to be over its three centuries of stupendous success. Subsequently, Bruno Latour has done much, controversially, to indicate the culturally relative nature of some of science's hardest facts.

Culture, in these dissolute circumstances, offered a treasure-house of observables to a discipline whose natural workplace was not a laboratory but more like an archaeological dig. Culture comprised the shards and droppings, and meaning was their crux. Solving the meaning, as it is usually put, is to be a matter of determining what the fragment (of a pot or of a social action) symbolizes. But symbolic meaning must be rather more intrinsic to the topic under scrutiny than attributed by the scrutineer. Certainly, all such attention in human enquiry both gives and takes, but insights will only tell such truths as transpire in answer to intelligently put questions. We discover what culture means in the systems of 'question-and-answer logic'.

The phrase is originally R. G. Collingwood's,[17] who invented it to describe his own archaeological methods while at work at Housesteads on the Northumbrian section of the Roman Wall. History, he claimed, is to be practised by historians as a matter of recovering the questions being asked of everyday experience by those historical actors for whom the action they settled upon was their answer. The difficulty with this is that, according to Collingwood's logic, the trick can only be brought off with successful answers to the original questions. A botched answer – a jug that will not pour, a discarded poem, a failed irrigation system, or a military defeat – remains unintelligible. The historian cannot recover from the answer (because it was not an answer) the questions the agent was asking, and cannot therefore think his or her thoughts again, thereby grasping the intention. The interpretation of intentions is the point of the whole business; as we all do with life all the time, we give sense to the world of experience by decrypting what we think other people are up to.

Thus Collingwood's pioneeringly common-sensible account of 'the science of human affairs'. It came in most handy for critics of old scientism, and the view that 'what you see is what you get', a method according to which the anthropologist knows all the answers, having anticipated all the questions. The new school, on the other hand, comprising such refusers of the old ways as Victor Turner, Marshall Sahlins, Meyer Fortes, Peter Worsley and Pierre Bourdieu (to whom we must return), joined with Clifford Geertz, hero of this chapter, not only in insisting upon the utter unalikeness of cultures (although not their incomparability), but also upon the facts of culture itself as being porous, blurred, intransigent to clarity of distinction, inconsistent and contradictory.

If that 'first real understanding' could have been attained no other way, and elementary understanding must be a product of reduction and simplification, such a natural sci-

entific precept will only apply so far. Simplify human experience too much in the interests of theorizability, and all you
get is banality. 'The anatomy of institutional structures' will
remain as dry and rattling a bag of bones as any other old
skeleton unless restored to breath and blood in the contexts
which originally gave it life. Only by speaking a spell of
artistry over it will the anthropologist be able to make it
walk, and this is only to be done by taking it back to its own
home. The singularity of the creature is then made more
visible less by giving it sharpness and clarity than by seeing
it through another optic, making the familiar strange and the
strange familiar, casting the cultural forms of one circumstance in the metaphoric figures of another.

V

The 'symbolism of action' was a name for the object of
enquiry first brought to academic attention by Kenneth Burke
in the 1940s. Burke was not caught up in any debate about
the definitions of culture, but he was a stern and early critic
of any too-confident distinction between subjectivity and
objectivity, and he also held the view that anthropology was
marking out quite new advances in the practice of the human
sciences, the subject-matter of which was, straightforwardly,
the culture and its vehicle, rhetoric.

Rhetoric, for Burke, was not a limitingly linguistic matter,
although it was surely a semantic one. Rhetoric took in
gesture (or, as people now say, 'body-language'), and
expressed motives. Burke entitled his trail-blazing book *A
Grammar of Motives*,[18] saying rather briskly that motives are
his shorthand for situations, before going on to identify his
situations as constituting the interminable drama of society.

'Dramatism', his key concept, Burke bequeaths to both historians and anthropologists, particularly Geertz. In an argument vividly recalling Collingwood, he wrote: 'In equating
"dramatic" with "dialectic" we automatically have also our
perspective for the analysis of history, which is a dramatic
process, involving dialectical opposition. *Every document
bequeathed to us by history must be treated . . . as the answer*

or rejoinder to assertions current in the situations in which it arose.'[19]

Burke's avowed intention was to disentangle the social drama according to the elements of action, scenery, purpose, agent and agency (best glossed as powers of autonomy as bestowed by the culture). These five points of his explanatory 'pentad' fuse in the drama, never more dramatic (and therefore symbolic) than at those 'strategic spots at which ambiguities necessarily arise'.[20]

Hence, Kenneth Burke's seeing all human behaviour as a comedy, which in turn demands a certain kind of fit between intellectual apparatus and temperament. For sure, comedy for him has the special, even peculiar, definition that it accrues 'the maximum of forensic complexity',[21] which I take to mean that comic vision finds as much argumentative contradictoriness in behaviour as possible. Burke's preference, he declares in his quirky way, is for 'the perspective by incongruity', one which, in counterposing itself to the grandeurs of tragic vision, sees evil as not so much satanic as stupid, identifies cruelty as shocking ignorance, and human misery as needless error. 'In sum,' he writes, '. . . the comic frame should enable people to be observers of themselves, while acting. Its ultimate would not be passiveness, but maximum consciousness.'

It is easy to attach such doctrines to the practice of anthropology and to use them to inspect the multitudinous details of life which may all be filed under culture. My purpose here with Burke to hand is to emphasize the culture which is of abiding interest to anthropologists as commonplace, domestic, both urban and rural, ambiguously eloquent of the experience it symbolizes, gossipy, saturated with use and meaning. If culture here connotes the old standby 'a whole way of life', then the way in question is as thronged, noisy, smelly, and as dense with complicated social rules and principles as possible.

Carrying home this great bag stuffed with culture, emptying it out in the study, the purpose of cogitation upon what it all means will be to make up a story by matching world-vision (or something like it, if somewhat less resonant) to this multiplicity of symbols – these funerary rites, marriage settlements, tips for baby-rearing, recipes, gardening hints, demon-deterrents, political leaflets, jokes, games and business deals – in such a way that they settle into their own, intelligible order. The anthropological visitor on our behalf arranges the facts according to the instruments, apportions the symbolic meanings which then become visible, and, planting those same meanings in time and place as neatly as possible, devises as true and full a story as possible out of the plot, its roles and characters, as have been made manifest.

This is only to put into the language of abstract theory those same processes which we all use to understand the banal and beautiful world as we move through it. Culture is, by this token, 'the ensemble of stories we tell ourselves about ourselves',[22] and the human scientist does no more than bring these stories to our imaginative attention, criticize them for falsehood, applaud them for their fidelity to life, rearrange or translate them to extend their intelligibility.

Theory explains; that is its purpose. The most elementary but always necessary kind of social theory may be found in proverbs, folktales, bedtime stories, myths, legends and locker-room anecdotes. Many may be the merest superstition – commonsense may be nonsense, folk-wisdom stupidity, the lessons of experience wholly misleading. But the stories we tell ourselves about ourselves carry instructions about how to live.

Nor are they always stories told by word of mouth. The stories which comprise culture are told commandingly, but as often as not in action and by example. The child learns by looking how to be good; how to be top; how to become student, lover, parent; stevedore, lumberjack, short-order cook; pillar of society or enemy of the people. The tales are as much embedded in the structure and texture of conduct as they are recounted to audiences orally, literally, cinematically, televisually. Culture moves through the rhythms, the images and words of the society's stock of stories, and its members dance and sing in and out of tune.

It gradually became the business of the human sciences to bring at least some of these stories up into the higher, drier air of abstraction and self-consciousness. This is the condition of modernity. The human sciences, for once in tandem with the natural ones, retrieve culture from nature, forever valuing self-awareness above happy unreflexivity, and doing so in the name of freedom and fulfilment. Michel Foucault,[23] redoubtably grim pessimist, saw in the process not freedom but enslavement, and in the extension of official knowledge about humanity the most powerful instruments ever confected for the imprisonment of passion and its reasons. But cheerfulness keeps breaking in on less contorted humanists, who profess the trade of teaching as many of humankind as will come to class how to turn experience into theory, enquiry into knowledge, and their consequences into the good society.

This happy-go-lucky formulation returns us to views of the new worlds, most of them pretty old, which anthropologists brought home. The news, we know, was of cultures, and the plural noun taught a singular lesson. It was the lesson of comparativism, and the exemplary teacher for our purposes is Clifford Geertz.

Geertz, supremely among anthropologists, insists on comparative method not just as anthropological stock-in-trade but as a moral and political necessity in so heterogeneous and jammed-in-on-itself kind of world. People may talk of globalization as though it were a smooth emulsion so painted over our differences that all social and economic life appears in the same colour. But the concept of cultures, let alone the lived variety of their embodiments, refuses the process. Whatever globalization may turn out to be in my last chapter, it is refracted, rebutted, repelled and reconstituted by cultures.

This being so, seeing (at least) double is a necessity for seeing anything. In our example, Geertz works in two more-or-less arbitrary, anyway contrastive, frequently inverted countries. His Morocco is dry, monotheistic, monarchic, Muslim, surrounded by desert and mountains except where it borders the Mediterranean; the French marked it copiously with their unmistakable imperial presence and the *marabout* preacher even more with his messianic and angry vehemence. Indonesia, vastly more populous (90 million people, 300 languages) is wet, once crowded with kings, and, since their abolition, poised always on the edge of civil war, Muslim on top of Hinduism and Buddhism with strong deposits left by Christianity and Communism. It comprises anything up to 3,000 islands, some of them empty of people, retains vestiges of Dutch rule, and might be rich if only it were not so poor.

Always to see one in the other, to observe bifocally, in one place to see figure as ground and in the other ground as figure, to veer from long to myopic vision, these are novel precepts in the human sciences; they emerge from a comparative method which has gone beyond the merely banal enumeration of presences here, absences there. There is no substitute for intelligence, but the comparison of cultures should of itself prevent too much Hegelian talk of world-historical nations, let alone everybody's strong inclination towards self-referentiality and the belief that their view of things is always the right one.

Intelligent envisioning, however, is the only stimulus of insight. Looking hard and seeing truthfully precede double vision. Anthropology and its historical sibling archaeology share the discipline of looking, the practice of old science. They cross into art, as we read plainly in the best practitioners, when they record what they see, and make it live again for their readers. Then they turn to their second subject – from Morocco to Bali, perhaps, or from Algeria to France, or even from Tennessee to New England – and the two pictures sit side by side, each razor sharp, each blurring the other.

VI

We need to have to hand an example of How to Study (a corner of a) culture in the style and manner advocated. Amid the admonitions to observe bifocally, to look through the different optics ground for us by the languages which distinguish one conceptual-cultural scheme from another, it is for a moment hard to know what to *do*. Following the sequence of cultural analysis by somebody incomparably good at it is, like reading a great poem or seeing a great painting, an epiphany. The strange is made familiar without losing any of its strangeness; analogues in one's own experience are quickened and changed by the sudden surprise of comparison; the vivacity and ardour of human commitment to the weird business in hand fairly grips us by the throat and heart, and shakes mind and its feelings into a new configuration. If we are lucky, such a rendezvous with other people's oddity leaves a keen, tender spot on our imagination. This is the stain of culture.

Clifford Geertz's 'Deep Play: Notes on the Balinese Cockfight'[24] is surely one of the most famous single contributions to the literature of anthropology, as well as being in itself a striking addition to English literature. It has its critics, most of them intent on convicting it of assorted unloadings of the burden of white man's condescension or misrepresentation or worse, but it is accessible to the commonest reader, vivid, pungent, moving, and profound.

It is also comic. The comedy – that 'maximum of forensic complexity', in Kenneth Burke's enigma – begins at the beginning. Newly arrived in Bali in April 1958, 'malarial and diffident', the Geertzes were blandly, politely but absolutely, refused any meaningful social encounters until, by happy accident, they attended a cockfight.

The cockfight was then illegal in Bali, but everywhere practised. Two eagerly living, not insubstantial creatures rip each other to bits with razors fastened to their heels. The illegality, the smell of blood and violent death, the likelihood of a bust by the cops, the implicit, inescapable jokes about men's cocks and cockfighting (but, by God, the dead seriousness of both), the noisy, excited, dusty gregariousness of it all, gives the traveller's tale terrific vitality, a whiff of prurience, and an object lesson.

The cockfight is duly raided by the police, the Geertzes run for cover like everyone else, are shielded by complete strangers, and are thereafter one of the family, getting to see plenty of cockfighting, cock-tending, cock-nurture, cock-worship:

> In the houseyard, the high-walled enclosures where the people live, fighting cocks are kept in wicker cages, moved frequently about so as to maintain the optimum balance of sun and shade. They are fed a special diet, which varies somewhat according to individual theories but which is mostly maize, sifted for impurities with far more care than it is when mere humans are going to eat it, and offered to the animal kernel by kernel. Red pepper is stuffed down their beaks and up their anuses to give them spirit. They are bathed in the same ceremonial preparation of tepid water, medicinal herbs, flowers,

and onions in which infants are bathed, and for a prize cock just about as often. Their combs are cropped, their plumage dressed, their spurs trimmed, and their legs massaged, and they are inspected for flaws with the squinted concentration of a diamond merchant. A man who has a passion for cocks, an enthusiast in the literal sense of the term, can spend most of his life with them, and even those, the overwhelming majority, whose passion though intense has not entirely run away with them, can and do spend what seems not only to an outsider, but also to themselves, an inordinate amount of time with them. 'I am cock crazy', my landlord, a quite ordinary *aficionado* by Balinese standards, used to moan as he went to move another cage, give another bath, or conduct another feeding. 'We're all cock crazy'.[25]

Crucial to the obliquity of perspective already commended is to understand how utterly unlike everyday Balinese decorum the crazily abandoned behaviour of the fight itself is. Animality to the Balinese is obscene; cockfights dramatize beastliness with shocking immediacy. As with all sports, there are intricate divisions of labour and indispensable experts – spurriers, handlers, umpires, and of course holders of the betting ring. The passion of gambling, the smell of blood, the flutter of torn feathers, the commitment of the (male) self, the rivalry of owners and villages and of mutual standing, catch up in a single whirl of good luck and bad the same mighty themes as do 'for other peoples with other temperaments *King Lear* and *Crime and Punishment* – death, masculinity, rage, pride, loss, beneficence, chance – and, ordering them into an encompassing structure, presents them in such a way as to throw into relief a particular view of their essential nature'.[26]

It is a bit of a shock to see Shakespeare and Dostoevsky put so coolly beside the fighting cocks. It is meant to be. It is anthropology's licence to be cavalier with categories. Art is both systemic across cultures and utterly peculiar to cultures. Its first use is 'to render ordinary everyday experience comprehensible by presenting it in terms of acts and objects which have had their practical consequences removed and been . . . raised to . . . the level of sheer appearances'.[27] Artforms are first of all a way of theorizing life without paying in blood or money (or, in the case of gambling, not much money). You may pay in tears, at the cockfight or at *La Travi-ata*, but not for long. Art gives form to a story about ourselves in which we can try out how things might have been otherwise, if only we had been or had met the heroine in the film or the novel.

In the cockfight as Geertz interprets it for us (and for the Balinese also), a people of unusual blandness and obliquity in ordinary dealings present a tale of themselves as wildly clamorous and murderously cruel. Like poems and symphonies, the cockfight is all passion and melodrama, and the gambler-spectators as well as the gambler-owners throw themselves into the fight with the grand gestures of Guignol, the masks of comedy and tragedy. What tragic actor, symphony conductor, and concerto pianist perform for us, they perform, with a little help from their cocks, for themselves.

Thus cockfights, puppet plays, renaissance frescos, football matches, and television drama alike present aspects of a people's subjectivity to itself, divided according to the groups and classes who use the form and the contents in question. That particular corner of the subjectivity may be dusty and unvisited or familiar and well swept, but, in *recognizing* it as a place for the moment to be, the audience not only view themselves, they remake themselves as well. The forms and contents of our cultural lives, heavy with feeling, are part of our constitution in all senses of the word.

For the Balinese, as in *all* other cases, the game is played within the thick, deep, and taken-for-granted assumptions and attire which make each kind of playfulness what they are. (Cockfights are, of course, for men only, and not any men but those with the status and the money to go in and play deep – lose from the depths of their pockets also, if need be.) What is really at stake are art's diverse forms and the uses to which it may be put in diverse times and places. Once there, the essential discriminations have all still to be made. The cockfight has extraordinary power: 'a dramatic shape, a metaphoric content, a social context'.[28] The cocks tear each other to bloody and feathery tatters and, doing so, dramatize a fight to the death between men-who-are-men, as well as, more immediately, prefiguring the social struggle for status (cocksureness) between both owners and gamblers. It is a story, a contained but disquietful story, which the Balinese make a florid and very expensive to-do about telling to themselves.

There are two principles to be observed from our ringside seat at the cock-fight, and they serve to underwrite this chapter. The first[29] is that any account of cultural behaviour must reach an understanding which would be, if one took proper care, intelligible to the performers of the behaviour themselves. Geertz's landlord, in other words, should have been able to find reasonable at least, intelligible certainly, and convincing potentially, Geertz's account of cock-fighting. (This should not be taken to mean that he would have to *agree* with it; he might withhold agreement because he could not follow it, or because some self-image or other was wounded, or out of sheer incredulity). This is one of the truths in relativism.[30]

The second principle returns us to comparativism. The philosopher Charles Taylor declares: 'other-understanding is always . . . comparative . . . we only liberate the others and "let them be" [as anthropology enjoins] when we can identify and articulate a contrast between their understanding and ours.'[31] Taylor characteristically derives these contentions from 'some deep intuition about the equal value of cultures'.[32] This is certainly not to say that the content of one culture may not be reproached for irrationality or inhumanity, but it is to claim for such egalitarianism a moral strength of its own, even where found incomprehensible or ridiculous by members of another culture. The study of the delicious profanity of cultures pulls in one direction towards localism (all cultures are equally valid in their own world) and in the other towards universalism (all cultures are judgeable according to standards of truth, virtue, beauty and rationality). Anthropology is poised always and waveringly on this fulcrum. Its definitions, descriptions and rich local instantiations of culture gave the concept an enormous geographical and historical reach which radically inflected the whole discourse of an age about the art of living. For it is the moral justification of the human sciences that they determine both how the world is and how it ought to be.

While anthropology, however, had more to find out and pass on, between 1918 and 2000 or so, about how the world *is*, a clutch of other enquirers, largely focused by the decidedly local study of English literature, set itself to speak a malediction over the profane culture it saw around it at home, and to criticize it according to the sanctities of the national imagination recorded in its best books and their noblest thoughts.

4
Culture and Redemption: Literature and Judgement

I

A national literature, George Orwell once remarked, is like a set of family jokes. Those on the inside know the old stories and recognize the favourite characters. Parents try to make sure that children become familiar with the family, that they will retell the jokes and introduce the characters to their children when the time comes. A national literature, like a repertory of family jokes, is also a mystery to the people on the outside, especially if they speak another language. Of course, *all* foreigners are dependably comic (including oneself when foreign), and a few of the best-known stories have travelled well enough to be counted one of the foreign family, so long as they are not too far away. (French, German and Japanese films and novels have, in limited numbers, made their way to Britain but very few Korean or Iranian ones.)

This being so, the authority of a national literature is a mixed business, half an occasion for the sort of affectionate reunion and arm-around-the-shoulders reminiscence which goes with family jocularity, half a dim, not uncommanding, venerable presence, and a source of both reassurance and admonition, of sibylline warning and cheerful advice. In Britain, English literature provides plenty of occasions in which those put down by those on top get something of their own back. At the same time, however, the intellectual habits of elite education in Britain, and the state nobility which it recruits and trains, have until very recently been such as to use the national literature as the 'house form' of social and political theory. (The contrast is with the French, whose graduates of the Écoles Normales run the country with a strongly political-theoretical cast of mind.)

Within this formation, English literature had all the seriousness as well as the repetitious conviviality of well-loved jokes. For the ruling class of the nineteenth century, the classical languages spoke in the autumnal accents of the patriarch, but the home literature in the tones of the nursery. Together they constituted the two key components of culture held in its interim definition by 1914: classical literature and its mighty cognates, the Law, the State, the Exchange, filled that part of culture which bestowed order and envisioned reason; national literature and its domain rooted in domesticity and privacy, the bathroom and the bedroom, shone out from that other part of culture which cherished and idealized the quotidian, the womanly, the passionate and the small. (You might say that this second part was what rescued John Stuart Mill from the first part, when, that is, he refreshed a soul made heavy as lead by the demands of public life and policy with the 'very culture of the feelings' to be drunk from Wordsworth's poetry.)

Between 1914 and 1918 both parts of the concept received the most terrible shock. The awful guardians of law and order had lawfully and in the most orderly way led millions to pointless and protracted deaths, while poetry had done little more than adorn the slaughter with rue or counterpose to its atrocity an abandoned wistfulness for the world which had been lost.

Perhaps not surprisingly it took a writer who came to both modes of culture from *outside* – the public and the private, the political and the cultural, the ideal and the actual – to envision the sheer impossibility of the retrieval of the world which had been lost by 1919. The great American poet, T. S. Eliot, more or less deliberately set himself to write the poetry and the books of cultural theory which would reconstruct an idea of culture adequate to a world gazing in such horror at what it had done in war and civil war between 1914 and his publication of *The Waste Land* in 1922.[1]

II

The Waste Land filled, as few poems have ever done, the intellectual and aesthetic space left open by the epoch for the advent not just of novelty but of moral diagnosis. It began, as well it might, from the lessons of anthropology in the first fifty years of the subject. Having read eagerly Jessie Weston's compression and redirection of Frazer's *The Golden Bough*,[2] Eliot framed his great poem, as is now well known, with the myth of the Fisher King, presented by Frazer as type and token of all ancient European symbolizations of the death of natural fertility in winter, and its resurrection in summer. The King becomes sterile; his knights search the iron-hard landscape for the sign of his successor, passing as they do so through the testing-places of the quest – the abyss, the perilous chapel, the unplumbed lake – until the King's successor (son of the godhead) declares himself, and sun and rain make their restorative return.

Eliot effects the most dazzling, learned and obliquely difficult retelling of the tale. After eighty-odd years of the poem, long after it has indeed become a family joke on either side of the Atlantic, it is hard at first to see it as so sparkling new (so funny and so solemn) as it first was when it was greeted, like so much modern art, with derision and angry detestation.

Eliot dramatizes the grand old myth by setting side by side fragments (his own word: at the end of the poem, the impersonal, unidentifiable prophet-poet declares, 'These fragments I have shored against my ruins') of the different versions of the fertility-and-resurrection stories, setting them to his highly personal prosody. Buddhism and Christianity (Christ's betrayal in the garden of Gethsemane, 'After the torchlight red on sweaty faces', the sudden image in the darkness coming at you like a film-shot), the haunting stories of Parsifal (Sir Percival) and of Arthur, flashes of historical splendour (Elizabeth and Essex) and of the long centuries in which destroying hordes rode hell-for-leather over the old bone-heap of Europe before coming to a dead stop in the trenches of the Somme – all these are glimpsed with frightening immediacy as the poem sweeps us just overhead, severed from time, looking through the eyes of God with a mortal sympathy.

It is a vision of almost complete pessimism, as well it might be at such a date. The pessimism is eased not at all by the mysterious and anonymous biographies from the present which recur through the poem: a voice dealing out the Tarot cards; a psychotic desperate for peace of mind, going out for a drive; a group of gossipy young working-class London women piling out of a pub at closing time, the prophet watching them, quoting with a too timely irony, 'Good-night, sweet ladies, good-night, good-night'; a grimly sexual seduction scene, doing nothing for fertility. Over the whole kaleidoscope, momentarily shaken into harmony instantly dispersed, plays the lost and noble music of an older order, its poetic rhythms and cadences ('When lovely woman stoops to folly', 'Sweet Thames, run softly till I end my song'), and its calm, implicit sanctioning of a culture situated in a benign and recurrent nature.

The Waste Land is an essay on cultural disintegration. What the poem does, in part by way of the half-dozen languages it speaks in, is *use* the idea of culture, by way of its contents, as the diagnostic measure of civilization, of human life itself, at least in its European heartlands and American dependency. These were the locations of world-history in 1922, and Eliot had read his Hegel. The world-spirit may have been advancing towards a condition of absolute reason during the nineteenth century, but the failure of politics to prevent such unprecedented warfare, and indeed the enthusiasm and efficiency with which politicians, military, industry, and the common people then pursued the performance targets of devastation, demanded a fuller explanation than human stupidity.

Eliot's answer was that if a culture no longer has natural, self-explanatory rhythms of life and death as expressed in the indispensable courtesies of a settled social order, it will destroy itself and the natural world. There were plenty of fellow artists, in paint (Picasso, Matisse), in music (Stravinsky, Berg), as well as in assorted literatures (Thomas Mann, Ezra Pound, D. H. Lawrence) saying the same thing and in comparably broken, deliberately distorted, anti-traditional forms.

But Eliot is probably the most succinct, possibly the most memorizable, certainly the most germane for our purposes. Eliot's theory of culture, as propounded in *The Waste Land*, went far deeper in the sensibility of anglophone readers than ever did his formal theorizations of 1945–6.

Eliot is much and piously blamed for a theory of culture, whether in his poems or prose, which (it is alleged) favours that half of the concept celebrating the purity of art in order to denigrate the routine squalor of life as lived by ordinary people. Perhaps it should be emphasized that his famous and notorious *Notes*[3] seem to be more-or-less directly addressed to widespread fears that Labour egalitarianism would attempt drastic modification of the British class system, admit free-place pupils to the public (private) schools, open the Universities of Oxford and Cambridge to wider social membership, and start to build a society in which talent and achievement would be the sole criteria of advancement. The old bromide, 'equality of opportunity', was new then.

Eliot thought poorly of it. Indeed, others, but further to the political Left, shared his misgivings. Michael Young, a boffin of social ideas who more or less wrote the Labour Party's election manifesto of 1945, published a polemic[4] to say how inhuman as well as how malfunctioning a society would be which was run on the principles, and by the membership, of a 'meritocracy' (Young's coinage). Eliot was, after all, by this time, and in his own words, a devout 'Anglo-Catholic in religion and royalist in politics'; he was also a patriot of the tourist side of England as seen by a highly intelligent, stiffly sentimental, decidedly bottled-up, chronically bored and timorously passionate mid-Westerner poet. The content of culture as he put it in the single best-known passage from the 'Notes' therefore 'includes all the characteristic activities and interests of a people: Derby Day, Henley Regatta, Cowes, the twelfth of August, a cup final, the dog races, the pin table, the dart board, Wensleydale cheese, boiled cabbage cut into sections, beetroot in vinegar, nineteenth century Gothic churches, and the music of Elgar'.[5] Sport, food, and art, the summer days out for the American tourist, each suffused with the aromas of the working or the ruling (but not the middle) classes. It was Raymond Williams who first pointed out the limitations of the choice, and

replaced various items with ones he preferred: committee procedure, the Trade Union movement, Lincoln cathedral.[6] After
all, Eliot himself terminated his register of favourites by
saying, 'The reader can make his own list', and the best pedagogic lesson from which the ambitious theorist of culture
could start is indeed to make a list of *a* people's culture
(preferably not one's own, or not to begin with). Culture, I
have said, is best thought of ostensively rather than definitionally, and Eliot's weakness in the 'Notes' is to lose what
The Waste Land and *Little Gidding* supremely realize, an
absolute fidelity of highly charged thought to the concrete
experience from which it must begin, and a complete refusal
of the ready-made, the boiler-plate or the factious in the
idiom and style of the poems.[7]

It cannot be said that the same virtues appear in the
'Notes'. Eliot's anglicized American sensibility is lacerated by
the idea of desecrating ancient Oxford quadrangles or allow-
ing the harmless slaughter of top-heavy gamebirds to be the
sport of poachers and plumbers as well as of those with prop-
ertied inheritances. More seriously, his Anglo-Catholic soul
recoils from so flagrantly *secular* a politics as would try to
engineer (still the put-down word of the day) a new sort of
culture.

Eliot is not, however, to be rebutted by our merely leaning
on the subsequent solidarities of social democracy, quoting
the *Notes*, and waiting for laughs. He starts by pointing out
that no sooner were the United Nations formally set up in
north Manhattan than they willed into being a junior organisation, UNESCO, whose very title assigned it responsibility
for cultural matters. Eliot's main premises are that culture
cannot be planned for as UNESCO intended; that it pertains
distinctly to three entities – individuals, groups and a whole
society; that it is larger than, hardly conscious of, but necessarily rooted in religion. Such beliefs, as he says, might be
formed out of an 'inferior or materialistic religion ["which
might blossom into a culture more brilliant than we can show
today"], a state of affairs nothing to do with the truth or
falsity of the beliefs in question but only proving that "any
religion, while it lasts, gives an apparent meaning to life, provides the framework for a culture and protects the mass of
humanity from boredom and despair".'[8]

Eliot dismisses Matthew Arnold's presumption that culture encloses religion, is more durable, and may be turned to redemptive account as secularization extends itself. In 1945 in Britain, the Arnoldians were out in force, trusting that even with a bankrupt Exchequer and the new arctic politics of the globe, art and the Arts Council, educational egalitarianism in the curriculum, and an assortment of culture-cultivating state bodies from the BBC to the British Film Institute, would raise the whole society to new levels of aesthetic fulfilment and suffuse 'the whole way of life of a culture' with the ideals of beauty, truth, and goodness.

It remains, for this writer at least, a noble ideal and a plausible programme. But it can only remain plausible if we take Eliot's objections seriously. One has to sideline his bad manners and clumsy wisecracks about Clement Attlee, and his argumentative sleight of hand (for example, the notoriously offensive *mot* about 'any passionate faith of the reader . . . [ha!] . . . who finds it shocking that culture and equalitarianism should conflict'). His most serious contribution to the accumulations of meaning and to the argumentative purposes of the concept is threefold.

First, Eliot insists on the joint meanings of culture as the repository of a society's ideals ('the storehouse of recorded value', in Leavis's phrase), and on the conception of the *ideal* as inseparable from the broader meaning of the word designating everyday life. Secondly, Eliot endorses with heart and mind the element in the concept which picks out Arnold's syllabus, Schiller's yearning, and Herder's affirmation of the potential value inherent in the life of each and any society.

Thirdly, and most rousingly, against the threats of debility and darkness, money-worship and the capture of culture by politics, he counterposed the ideal of great poetry and its sustaining tradition, each practicable only because of a community of languages – ultimately, a world of poetry – within which different poets write and, quite unknowingly, make possible the new poetry of some other language. 'Whenever a Virgil, a Dante or a Shakespeare is born, the whole future of European poetry is altered.'[9]

This is Eliot on culture militant and at his most sympathetic, writing directly out of his experience as a poet. The artist in any medium works with his or her urgent, competitive, and daunted sense of what other such artists have done or are doing. Culture renews itself, *or is debilitated*, by the work in hand. It's quite a responsibility. (Those artists who do not see it so, he rightly implies, are beneath contempt, although of course they may do damage.) Bearing it can only be made tolerable if the artist in question retains an accurate enough scale with which to judge the art in question. Doing so on behalf of the culture, the citizen-artist is appointed custodian of judgement on the present, and keeper of the vision of the good society on earth, suitable candidates being assigned to and assuming the role in the social structure of imaginative redeemer.

Eliot, and that powerful tradition in Britain which followed his lead and pungently dissented from it also, stuck to this account of artistry, given its outline by the great Romantics. It remains so compelling precisely because it is still part of our social reality: even at this present money-saturated, celebrity-sodden moment in artistic life, art is expected to provide or imply a picture of the finest life it knows. This is so even when the lives it tells of are hideous to see: told with bleak or frenetic truthfulness they take the measure of how far they fall from grace, and grace can only be realized in a non-theistic society in terms of those best values of the present re-embodied for an imaginable future. The fierce criticism by Eliot's heirs in England – the line of F. R. Leavis, Raymond Williams, and Richard Hoggart – of the way of life that they saw around them carries weight because, as part of the intelligentsia, they occupy the neighbour role to the artist and artists join intellectuals in criticizing the present against the best that may be imagined of and for the future.

So Eliot's argument is not to be dealt with as lightly as some do who take political offence at only passingly offensive remarks. What riles his opponents on the Left is his assumption that for a society to produce a serious culture, there must be a close and necessary relation between its ruling class and its elite producers of culture, and that both must be sustained by a sufficiently long-lived tradition of mutual if arm's-length respect.

Put with that degree of mild abstraction, this is unexceptionable. Culture must have practitioners who are *very good*, and they must, to count in the way of life of the society, stand near enough beside political power, neither in its pocket nor behind its back. Culture (to put it a bit blankly) also needs among its practitioners those who work from below, who practise subversion, and, in the commonplace designating the duty of intellectuals, 'speak truth to power'. But that is the point: dissenting versions of culture must be audible; the old avant-garde shocked the bourgeoisie and disconcerted the official pose of political power. In doing so, it changed, however slightly, the figures upon the cultural ground.

III

The connection between culture and politics, as chapter 2 demonstrated, is blurred and complex. In turn, the final chapter will be concerned with admonishing culture for its presumption and emphasizing with suitable stringency the thin lines of the political redoubt. Eliot was busy at the same work, and, however uncongenial his commitments and disingenuous his rhetoric, he provides us with a practical (rather than a theoretical) sociology whose main principles are as follows: culture is differentially located in the individual, the group and the whole society; it cannot be planned for in the latter; it holds in tension the ideal and the real, desire and actuality; elite culture and political power may be coterminous but should never be synonymous; the making of culture by elites and by the people ('folk' would be Eliot's word) is transformed over time into the collective tradition of the society; such a collective work as culture is does not stop at national frontiers. These principles compose a theory, however Eliot would have disliked such a charge.

The man who followed his lead most forcefully, first in Britain and then in the debate about culture at large, would have denied theoretical ambitions with much greater ferocity. F. R. Leavis stands indeed for the absolute refusal of theory as itself the lethal carrier of narrowing of the mind and petrifaction of the spirit. In bearing the standard of culture so publicly, Leavis followed the lead of those for whom culture, simply defined as the art of living, would be a weapon with which to castigate what he described as 'technologico-Benthamite civilization'.

The phrase itself was elaborately contrived. 'Civilization', in the history of our argument, has until recently been an approbatory word; now Leavis measures the depth of its damnation by including the whole of its social achievement in its ambit. The circumlocution avoids using the word 'capitalism' for fear, first, of being counted amongst the company of anti-capitalists and therefore of socialists, and, secondly, in order to identify not a political but a cultural entity, and one in thrall to machine-worship and the fixity of that social calculus which refuses to acknowledge any human feature unamenable to quantification. Politics, for Leavis, was irrevocably corrupted. The cultural domain was the moral domain, and in the teeth of a degraded civilization, the only salvation and grounds for affirmation could be found in the lives of certain exceptionally creative spirits, mostly writers: Shakespeare, Blake, Dickens, D. H. Lawrence: the vitality and the grace discernible in their writing could irrigate these spirits parched by utilitarianism, and quicken them to new life in dark times.

It doesn't sound much to bet on. It was the best Leavis could find. But it is hard to communicate the extraordinary force, the entire lack – until his three last and silent years before his death in 1978 – of desperation, the terrific *fight* and the exquisite and detailed delight with which he made his local affirmations on behalf of culture.

Leavis brought Eliot's account of culture into incomparably more vivid and pervasive a context. It lived, of course, not merely in the blazing individuality of this or that writer; the writers were what they were by virtue of the civilization (this time used as ratification) which made them and was itself made by many people. This was his pedagogic point. His prophets spoke for and from a people (the English people) who could call their culture their own.

Put like that, it is a programme at whose heart is not so much the open sea of culture as the schoolhouse of education. Indeed, Leavis wrote a school textbook[10] with his schoolteacher friend and ally Denys Thompson, in which he provided for bright students a casebook of quotations indicating on the one hand what it was like to live in a culture which resulted in an art of living and therefore constituted a community, and on the other illustrating the utter loss of these qualities in a modern society which lived as it did in the wastelands of modern suburbia (here rather brutally characterized by extracts from an empirical study of the small Connecticut township of Middletown).

There was an exuberance and high-spiritedness about this splendid, slightly unhinged little book which belies its reputation today. Leavis himself invented the advertising copy by way of illustrating the dreadful damage such an idiom did to public truthfulness. The book was sprinkled with his favourite quotations; the questions, to put it mildly, led students in only one, the right direction. But in commemorating what he called 'the organic community' (which he found in the doubtless idealized but none the less actually lived reminiscences of one George Sturt,[11] who owned and ran a wheelwright's business for many years during the last decades of the nineteenth century in Farnham, Surrey), Leavis followed the rhetorical device familiar to us from Carlyle and William Morris, whereby an ideal social order from the past is reimagined by way of bringing sharply into relief present absences and degradations.

Leavis was never backward in giving hostages to fortune. His ideal communities, in which culture coincided with membership, art with life, included the little river-station in the Mississippi described in Mark Twain's novel *Pudd'nhead Wilson*; the historically actual training ship *Conway*, upon which Joseph Conrad served his indentures for the Mercantile Marine; John Bunyan's actual congregation around his dissenting church in seventeenth-century Elstow, Bedfordshire, and D. H. Lawrence's mining village, Eastwood, in early twentieth-century Nottinghamshire.

D. H. Lawrence became, over the span of Leavis's career, his touchstone case for trying out his beliefs and judgements about the losses and disruptions of his lifetime, and it is in his advocacy and exposition of Lawrence's *œuvre* that Leavis most brilliantly locates a representative genius in the process of a *cultural* formation without some knowledge of which the work is only partly to be understood.[12] Leavis speaks indeed of our 'immeasurable good fortune' that Lawrence was born in 1885 and into that singular society and geography. It was just the moment when members of an only recently self-discovered working class came to a proud enough consciousness of themselves as such. They remained countrymen enough to know in detail their wild and garden flowers and vegetables, to keep their bees and scraps of farmland, to move in and out of the remnants of an agrarian way of life, all at the same time as they organized themselves both with and against the dangerous, not-badly-paid-until-you-were-laid-off, fraternal life of pitmen, and the monstrous arbitrariness of demand for coal.

Refusing the language of class warfare as the English academic classes did in those days freed Leavis from any need to acknowledge the contemporary simple-mindedness of Marxism, and left him under no Party obligations to name the Lawrence family as members of an oppressed proletariat. Thus he can describe the local culture and domestic way of life as intensely civilized in terms of its natural piety (the Nonconformist churches), the seriousness and relevance to living of its education (the Miners' Institute Library, the then University College, Nottingham, and the passion for poetry, however uneven in quality, which Lawrence recollects of his mother and among cultivated local friends both in letters and in *Sons and Lovers*),[13] the closeness of its work to its home and of both to hardship and sudden death, the natural mutuality of the working poor, always braced for the heart-stopping, whooping blast of the pit-head alarm.

Leavis contrived from Lawrence and the other great writers with whom he shared his abundance of life, and his passion for its transmission to those readers who could hear him ('minority culture'), what one of his own intellectual sons and heirs called 'a knowable community'. Perhaps it is a mark of what Leavis knew was lost, that such a community was peopled entirely from the written word.

For, when Raymond Williams coined the concept, he also was writing about novelists, those same novelists from Dickens to Lawrence who contrived for *their* readers a 'knowable [but imaginary] community' with its familiar characters, corners, streets and homes – its culture, indeed – with which they could help repair the blankness and disjunctures, the cruelty and want, the sheer unknowability of the monstrous industrial city, destroying, reinventing and tearing into life all around them. To Williams's mind, this was what Leavis was doing as he battled in the core of his being – no academic objectivity even to be attempted here – with what Williams also named as his 'overwhelming, at times overwhelmed' sense of deep chasms and tumultuous crises in culture.

Alongside his sometime teacher and colleague, and in his no less intense disagreements with him, Williams's extraordinary empathy brings out the *self-made* nature of so much of that culture which Leavis used to indict the enemy: 'technologico-Benthamite civilization'. If his selection of culture-reviewing writers is an example of culture as earthing and transforming itself in an individual receiver, it may also presage the *radical individualization of cultural repertory* which marks our present.

Leavis's work is the strongest reminder we have that culture is best defined ostensively (pointing and saying 'there!') and that, for all that the vital crux ('vital' in the sense of both vivacious and indispensable) is life as lived individually, individuals are each and all the sociable product of culture, and culture as lived and living (or maimed and dying) in everyday language.

The significance of this lifelong meditation on life and death in culture turned on the acuteness and inevitability of its representatives. Leavis's imagination and being were seized by the grand topics sailing down the mainstream of English intellectual life immediately before and during his lifetime. He dealt with them, and those writers who represented them, with a rare radicalism, marshalling their support for his revulsion from all that was phoney, arrogant, money-fixated, coldly inhuman, cruelly neglectful in British social life (and there was plenty of all that), throwing himself passionately into the fight against insincerity, against a general failure to grasp the real, to refuse cliché in either living or language, to betray what in that fine phrase he called 'the inevitable creativeness of ordinary everyday life'.

This was his cause and it split open the conventions of scientific objectivity and judicious empiricism which were supposed to contain the human sciences. Leavis's careering through culture teaches a three-part pedagogy, and inaugurates the still-fledgling effort to make the critical-creative study of culture the birthright of all citizens. In the first part, he teaches that understanding culture demands an utter seriousness of purpose, a capacity to surrender oneself to the transformative power of a work of art, and a complete sincerity, the same thing as a perfect truthfulness. The second lesson teaches that *everything* signifies value and meaning (some horrible, some bountiful, none assumable in advance), that these may be discovered by exacting scrutiny (the title of Leavis's quarterly literary journal) and by sympathetic searching-out, and that making judgements as accurate as possible is a spontaneous necessity as well as a human responsibility. Thirdly, Leavis tells us that while culture must live in individual lives, it is collectively made and that collective and creative making is the ground of human being.

IV

This last is the emphasis which, in spite of Leavis's crazy politics and violent prejudices, his ignorance of so much (pharmacology, say, or welfare economics) which we would count gratefully as a beneficent part of modern culture, still commends to us his fine intransigence, his courage, his tenderness towards domestic values. These were also the qualities in relation to thought about culture which gave their lead to the two other giants of cultural theory who cannot be omitted from this brief British history of the uses of culture as concept and as social medicine.

The two thinkers in question are Raymond Williams and Richard Hoggart, and, although they lead in rather different directions, it is something of a truism to note their similarities.[14] Both were born into the working class. Hoggart was an orphan raised in extreme but unself-pitying penury by his grandmother, who then died when he was seven (in 1925); Williams the only child of a steadily employed railway signalman in a village in the border country of Wales and England. Both were phenomenally intelligent and confident schoolboys who won scholarships to the best local secondary (grammar) schools and university – Leeds for Hoggart, Cambridge for Williams. Both absorbed an ineradicable politicization in a humane and traditional socialism from their origins in the culture from which such beliefs came in the first place. Finally, both men went to war in 1940, Williams to tanks, Hoggart to heavy guns, and both lived through that powerful, moving and bloodless revolution whereby British working-class civilians, temporarily in the uniform of the military or munitions or medical staff or all the dozens of outfits – khaki, blue or mufti – in which a people fought the first all-nation war in history, came out of it determined that their bit of the world really would be a better place, with fewer of the far-too-rich in it and enough work, free doctors, fair shares, kindly schools, decent bathrooms.

Hoggart's two great books, divided by some thirty years and public duties which prevented his publishing a great deal of his own in the interval, testify to that large historical achievement, and do so, as Leavis's did, by bringing new and unexpected values into the intellectual clearing. People speak sometimes of 'class' values, and the working or ruling class as proprietors of these. But in fact there are only values themselves, although there are certainly material and class circumstances which foster certain values at the expense of others.

In *The Uses of Literacy*,[15] one of the now-classical textbooks of method in the study of culture, Hoggart makes daringly explicit something unexpressed but unquestioned in the British debate on culture since Matthew Arnold. He takes the patient exposition of meaning in literary study, the careful teasing-out of dependable moral conclusions, and he straightforwardly applies them to the values, the language, and the symbolic actions of everyday life.

In this, he becomes, one might say, a Geertzian anthropologist in the home society. In his case, however, he is not translating from exotic actuality to intelligible metaphor, rather he is reading as closely as possible something familiar to him all his life (for it *is* his life). He is then directing the attention of his own class *and* the class for whom these facts of life are novelties towards the strengths both have been taught to ignore but none the less depend on, as well as towards the famine which threatens them such that if they are lost (and they have been by now) they will prove irrecoverable.

Many of Hoggart's critics, never more so than on the sanctimonious outer feathers of the Left wing, have pointed out that in the details of the book he concentrates, like Eliot, on the cultural contents of working-class food, speech, songs, and art rather than working-class work and politics. Now Hoggart was hardly a newcomer or a tourist in the country he travelled. Rather, he describes what he encountered as a child (since his work promoted him out of his class), one raised without a father, and in omitting politics he not only followed the usual definitions of culture but also the habitual convention of British domestic life in any class. Hoggart, unflinching in his political commitment, has not been forgiven by some for staying at home with the homely and, as it happens, with the Labour Party.

Like much obtuse criticism, this is too hard. For Hoggart did so much with home and its faithful family of cognates, community, neighbourliness, mutuality. Home, one might pointedly add, is the one political concept for which most people are likely to risk death; but one looks in vain for a study of it on the shelves of political theory.[16] Hoggart is our counter-example: not of the missing political theorist, but of the thinker who finds in the unself-conscious meanings of everyday practices *the signs of life*. These signs live in culture and are, from time to time, picked out and silhouetted as political values over which class or national warfare may be waged, legislation ruled upon, manifestos declared. Such signs are the very stuff of happiness or misery, and politics no more than the quarrels one has to have from time to time over what to do with them.

One of Hoggart's finest passages, from the heart and stomach of his childhood, tests the meanings of working-class home food in the early 1930s. It bears extended quotation.

> 'Something tasty' is the phrase in feeding: something solid, preferably meaty, and with a well-defined flavour. The tastiness is increased by a liberal use of sauces and pickles, notably tomato sauce and piccalilli. I used to notice that in the flusher early years of married life my relatives were often frying at teatimes – chops, steaks, kidney, chips . . . The emphasis on tastiness shows itself most clearly in the need to provide 'something for tea', at weekend if not each day. There is a

great range of favourite savouries, often by-products – black puddings, pig's feet, liver, cow-heel, tripe, polony, 'ducks', chitterlings (and for special occasions, porkpies, which are extremely popular); and the fishmonger's savouries – shrimps, roe, kippers and mussels . . . At the weekend we lived largely like everyone else except the very poor, and Sunday tea was the peak. By six on that evening, the middens up the back had a fine topcoat of empty salmon and fruit tins. Pineapple was the most popular because, in that period of what now seems extraordinarily cheap canned fruit, it could be bought for a few pence (there was a recurrent story that it was really flavoured turnip). Peaches and apricots were more expensive and needed something approaching an occasion – a birthday or a sudden visit by relatives from a few miles away. The salmon was delicious, especially the red middle-cut. I still find it far 'tastier' than fresh salmon.[17]

Hoggart's equable Yorkshire voice plays over the items of food: the value of 'tastiness' does all his work for him. Without having to descant upon tastiness as concealing cheap meat or as a key quality in hard-working lives without much opportunity for flavour or colour, he can list with that enviable ease of manner and unsentimentally loving recollection the individual dishes so that they speak with a silent eloquence of what they meant in hard-won generosity, the duties of family hospitality, the timeless human pleasure in plenitude, the ancient ceremony of food and table, the gregariousness of home at weekends, Monday morning at 5 a.m. still a safe night's sleep away.

Square meals do no more than offer a glimpse of all Hoggart means by culture and how he evaluates it. For this hearty celebration is only half his story. In the second part of his great book, he traces by way of the culture – its reading in newspapers, magazines and thriller fiction, its leisure life as lived in amusement arcades, coffee bars, *palais de danse*, its turns of speech and the imaginative life it drew from the early years of postwar mass broadcasting – what he sees as a marked decline in the strength of character of his class, of the uprightness of its inner life, the robustness of its manners and of the steadiness of its 'civil affections' (in David Hume's fine phrase). He describes the process as an 'unbending of the springs of action'.

Almost fifty years after the book came out, it is hard not to think he was right. His is far from a Leavisian history of degradation, nonetheless. He puts great faith in the canonical virtues of an active, critical, and wide-awake citizenry and in the necessity for its members to oppose, dissent from, and to watch out for the great minotaur of capitalism and all that it makes for our delight and destruction. At the same time, in for instance his little portrait of the Farnham where he lived for twenty-five years[18] (the same town that was home to George Sturt's wheelwright's shop), he speaks up for those values which ensure the continuity of English culture and the moving way in which he finds them embodied on the streets of a wealthy market town a short train ride from London.

It is, however, in his noble autobiography[19] that he reviews his life's work in the theorization, teaching and administration of culture (he was for some years an Assistant Director-General of UNESCO in Paris). It is an unelegiac, powerfully celebratory and intellectually steely book, and it gives the lie to those high-IQ morons of a British Marxist persuasion who configure Hoggart as a has-been Left-Leavisite. Leavis, as we noted, projected the flame of his being against the culture of the day; he battled to defeat rotten with ideal culture. He counted himself defeated but not failed. Hoggart, by contrast and even in the sturdy independence of his old age, was intent on naming the corrigible monstrosities of latter-day culture, commending all that had been gained by way of independence and comforts, enlargements of freedom and chances of happiness, and mourning what had been lost of the civic virtues and the tradition of solidarity. It is a simple, often-repeated travesty to claim that Hoggart follows Leavis in regrets for the disappearance of the old organic community,[20] while moving its last time and place from the English Home Counties and the Nottinghamshire mining towns of 1885 to the up-and-down, long-ribbed working-class terraces of 1930s Leeds.

Hoggart's case is much more balanced than that. It is that mass broadcast and commercial culture loosens, starves, and attenuates the thick actuality of a culture as lived in its local knowledge and accent. If they have their strengths, they are not that of the locality, or of settled habitation and membership.

V

As it happened, his powerful coeval, Raymond Williams, also in the business of defining and establishing culture as both precise and respectable enough to provide the content of academic enquiry, was writing his own first classic on the subject at the same time as Hoggart wrote *The Uses of Literacy*, and while working in the same sort of job.

Williams was a tutor in what used to be called the extra-mural department of a university, meaning, literally, that its classes took place away from the formal centre and main buildings and, in practice, that the classes accepted students of all kinds of ability, were largely conducted without contributing to an academic degree or award, had a voluntary enrolment and a syllabus fixed more or less by the tutor and approved, on the whole readily, by the regional organizer (sometimes the same person). Hoggart's university in the job was Leeds,[21] Williams's Oxford.

Williams completed his English degree at Cambridge when he returned from his Guards Regiment tank in 1945. Leavis then dominated English studies, and strongly as Williams declared himself drawn to Leavis's ardent intensity, moral seriousness, and the wide historical range (though always within English history) of his field of judgement, he no less strongly rejected Leavis's certainty that the organic community had been dissolved by history, as Williams also did the nature – the class nature – of Leavis's redemptive texts, and the vision which enclosed them.

It was not that Williams did not admire Blake, Dickens or Lawrence. All of them lived life with a fine devilishness and fight, an outspoken detestation of English bourgeois and ruling-class hypocrisy, an independent gaiety of spirit and an unstoppable garrulity. What Williams would have none of was the idea that if you did not endorse Leavis's sacred texts and share exactly in the rhythms by which the relevant judgements were made you were spurned as not of the elect, in a movement of class shunning essentially identical to all other such exclusions in English social life. Not admiring Lawrence was, in Williams's caustic view of the Leavisites, like not wearing the right clothes.

So Williams stood for the reality of the 'organic community' along the railway line at Pandy, just north of Abergavenny, and wrote his first novel[22] to prove it was there. As we saw in chapter 1, he traced the genealogy of the concept of culture in British intellectual life, returning to it time and again[23] in order to feel the force of that enervating nostalgia which had been irresistible in British 'structures of feeling' for a century and more.

'Structure of feeling' was Williams's own conceptual coinage and suggested a way of understanding how our experience of culture is formed and made graspable by our building a way to accommodate it with our feelings. To describe this little piece of architecture on behalf of a group or a society is, as chapter 5 proposes, to go a long way towards harvesting the field of cultural production. Emotions grasp the subject of experience. If they change, the significance of the experience changes. This often happens. Culture teaches us our feelings and is the only source of our experience. Grasping an experience and being fully alive in and to the culture is the same thing. The only chance I have of full insight is comprehensive feeling: my cognitions are at the behest of the best feelings and attitudes I can have, relevant to the subject in hand.

Williams on Lawrence is a particularly pure example of the good man talking about the culture which counts for good. Unlike Leavis, Williams does not see Lawrence's blazing individuality of self, but the depth of his commitment to others, in sickness or in health, in quarrelsomeness or in tenderness. In this he avows the boldest as well as the most veeringly uncertain of the disciplinary maxims of Cultural Studies, the academic subject which becomes one slow consequence of cultural analysis. Identifying rather than comparing himself with others, Williams can speak as he does because of an absolute trust in the human representativeness of his own experience.

This is a critique of culture nonetheless, and then of the politics configured on its ground. Williams's early attacks on capitalism, in the long last section of *Culture and Society* and throughout its 1961 sequel, *The Long Revolution*, assailed the routine cultural practices and values which made Britain as it then was. The pietistic and overdone respect of class society for 'individuality', the ambiguous deference to class, the dull acquiescence in shocking disparities in pay, the permission given to custom and state to exalt market forces and property rights over minimum expectations of shelter and safety, all these Williams arraigned in 1961 as politically remediable, no doubt, but culturally generated and sanctioned.

Culture and Society reviewed his forebears, adduced the key bibliography of British thinkers on the subject, and initiated Williams's full-blown critique of the shortcomings of British society from within that structure of feeling which raised and made him and which also made it possible to think of socialism not only as a political and legislative programme for a juster and more equal society, but as picturing a pattern of human relationships conducive to the art of living. This is what it is to invest the treasure of your past in your hope for the future.

As the years are apt to do, they told upon Williams's optimism if not his prodigality. By 1983, as he anticipated the millennium, he had watched the coming-to-power of a quite new breed of buccaneer-capitalist and seen also, with grim horror and no surprise, its enlistment of ready recruits from the ranks of official politics (not to mention academics). This, it may be, is the moment at which culture-in-the-neutral-sense may be said to merge with politics. The mutual dissolution has long been noticeable in the United States, long flagrant in Italy. Nor is this a little matter of corruption; it is a lethal blending of political and therefore coercive power with the everyday value-assumptions – what Charles Taylor calls the 'strong evaluations' – of the culture. It is as though all the symbolism of a society is to be printed as money: art, religion, the customs of the country and the gestures of street and office.

Writing from the land of what William Cobbett (himself a sturdy contributor to early nineteenth-century descriptions of a common culture) once called 'Old Corruption', Williams projected his critique onto a world stage with a global plot. The villains were the architects of 'Plan X', the irresponsible wielders of power whose objective was always 'temporary competitive advantage within a permanent and inevitable danger', a danger he saw that same power élite[24] as happily working up by suppressing labour difficulties and ensuring that organized dissent was as ineffectual and widely derided as possible:

> For this is percentage politics, and within its tough terms there is absolute contempt for those who believe that the present and the future can be managed in any other way, and especially for those who try to fudge or qualify the problems or who refuse the necessary costs. These wet old muddlers, like all old idealists, are simply irrelevant, unless they get in the way.[25]

Thus far Williams is writing biting but straightforward politics. But the dissenting heroes and heroines of his global plot are not exactly political actors in the usual sense. They express certain broad cultural surges of popular feeling which, in the emasculation of citizenhood of the time, are carefully run off by the mastodons of official power into the secure channels and containers constructed to hold opposition and protest in hygienic isolation: the Sunday march to Trafalgar Square, the pickets behind the police railings at municipal or corporate offices, the amateur broadsheets and academic maledictions. The modes of political dissent are by these tokens cultural: the spectacle (street theatre); the personal (demonstrations); the archaic (the leaflet, the banner); the mildly-insurrectionary (paint-throwing, window-smashing, police-baiting). Their cultural form ensures that their political content can only impinge on real politics when culture itself expands to overflow its limits and inundate politics. At that point, the social order breaks down until such time as the boundaries between culture and politics are re-established.

Williams steps back from his bitter political summary with a useful piece of theorizing, one which makes it possible to see how his ruthless buccaneers get away with it. In a simple temporal model, he identifies[26] three value-components of culture, as being the residual, dominant and emergent (past, present and future). All are contemporaneous and all competitive. When a value slips from dominant to residual, that is not necessarily final; people may successfully reinstate it. When a new value begins to emerge, it may nonetheless prove abortive, and after a while disappear. Certainly, dominance may be challenged when it transpires that values dominant with the architects of Plan X are too much to stomach in the larger culture.

When this is so, as Quentin Skinner sharply reminded Williams,[27] the tough talkers *cannot* simply dismiss the old idealists as irrelevant. Even very rich and powerful members of the élite must win some kind of popular support from that inconstant but not ignoble fiction, public opinion. To do so, they must adopt certain ruses to transfigure culture in their cause. To take one contemporary and pressing concern for a culture, the condition of nature herself as poisoned and distorted by culture, the hard men have to acknowledge the likelihood of ecological danger, but redescribe their enterprise in such a way as to accommodate the objectors. They may say that the case of (say) global warming is still unproved; they may point out that poor nations can only catch up with rich ones by continuing with industrialization and that this needs to be achieved first if poverty is to be eradicated and there is to be any chance of international agreement on what to do next; they may say that only technological developments are capable of controlling and repairing the deformations of nature they have already caused.

Certainly, they may also bear ruthlessly on their destructive course. Then dominance must collide with emergency, and there is no saying who will win. Even half-forgotten or residual values may then have their day, as environmentalists make appeal to an ancient comity of nature with culture such as the ideal social orders of history may have enjoyed in one or other Garden of Eden. Such an appeal may earth itself in the resources of the culture where the energy of all such tales is deposited, glowing a little in the veins of its morphology. Residualists with old banners and emergents, bristling with new values, alike call up ghosts of past and future in order to connect their case to 'the best that has been known and thought' by their culture.

VI

Each of our four worthies in this chapter is there to illustrate the textbookish lesson that our favourite concept of culture

derives its meanings from its use, and they have continued to
deploy the triple meanings which accrued in the nineteenth
century while using the term for their quite new purposes.
Thus Eliot is at pains to draw upon the idealizing realm of
culture as well as to confirm its contents from the everyday
– boiled cabbage, Wensleydale cheese and so forth. But in
the elaborate persona of English gentleman and publisher,
man of letters and devout communicant, he tried to fuse
together the profanity of culture with the sacredness of
religion, the family joke of literature with the changeless
liturgy of worship.

Eliot's argument about culture no longer has a central place
in any such discussion, for all those of his assertions which
remain valid. As George Steiner pointed out (beginning, rightly
enough, 'Not an attractive book'),[28] to discuss the topic at that
date without even mentioning the extermination camps was
more than a little parochial, and Steiner went on in an excess
of self-mortification to make much of the undoubted fact that
the majesty of German culture had apparently done nothing
to mitigate the worst of German atrocities. Camp adjutants,
or so he claims, listened to Schubert before checking the
throughput of the afternoon incineration.

We do not have to pitch our voices quite so high in
nonetheless agreeing that in his prose, at least, Eliot is too
lofty, as well as silently but intensely too partisan, to serve as
a current guide to culture. We admit him for his thickening
of the concept and for the sumptuousness of his poetic diag-
noses, but Leavis offers more to admire and, even at his spiki-
est and most prejudiced, to warm to. Of course, he flouts the
rules of human science; he is emphatically not detached,
objective, aspiring upwards to the view from nowhere. He is,
however, notably judicious (which may give us pause to
doubt our own blessed objectivity); he is comprehensive in
feeling, he gives himself to the fragment of culture before him,
and in being so unself-protective, it might be argued, recoils
with greater revulsion from what he cannot bear than does a
warier observer like Raymond Williams.

But Hoggart's and Williams's objections to Leavis's iden-
tifications and theory of culture stand. Their strongest
objection was personal and did not have to be spoken: the
judgements which his theory yielded utterly derogated the

culture from which each man came. They had both lived in strong communities with their own expressive speech, a striking richness of custom and ceremony in strikingly penurious circumstances, lively and gregarious forms of leisure, together with codes of courtesy, moral conduct (and jocularity) a great deal preferable to some of the more rarefied saloons of well-upholstered civilization.

Putting things so robustly is a reminder that such cultures had a politics and a political party. For the English middle classes, particularly after the debacle of the First World War, politics was sundered from morality, and thereafter moral insight trumped political commitment.

Hoggart and Williams would have none of that, and indeed one way of seeing their two lives is as working-class representatives promoted by virtue of their gifts, but also by virtue of the democratic energies released by the Second World War. That war was universally agreed to have had a moral and political point, to have almost been lost before it started because of ruling-class evasions, cowardice and hypocrisy, and was now the indisputable justification for creating a more equal society. The two men pledged themselves to hold up the best lights of the culture they had learned at home *and* the one they had learned at university. In Hoggart's case he was committed to nurture the cause of both cultures as one of the world's senior cultural bureaucrats, a rare example of the practice of that misleading cliché, 'cultural politics'. Williams's purpose, on the other hand, was to catch the configuring of politics upon the stuff of culture, and to estimate the weight of each in the other's forms. Form was the crux. In a noble professorial address, he cast the form of our contemporary culture, like Kenneth Burke, as drama,[29] and our culture as best interpreted through a dramaturgy. In saying this, he acknowledged the extraordinary degree to which received drama dominates all our cultural lives, and saw, shadowed in the endless play of those scripts and images, the conversation of a culture with itself, 'talking not to but past others', nobody quite finishing what they have to say, anxious, fractious, apprehensive, enclosed in little rooms in a crisis of an inexpressible sort, waiting for the shout in the street which will be a sign of what is going to happen to them next.

Hoggart, unpersuaded by Marxism that emancipation awaited its revolutionary moment, shared the same sense that broadcasting was to constitute mainstream culture from 1960 or so onwards. His was the main hand to draft the major government policy statement (the Pilkington Report) which, if effected fully at that date, would have made the context for creative work in radio and television much more fully democratic as well as more cultivated. Pilkington did, of course, make a difference. But Hoggart's place here beside Williams is as radical rewriter of our concept, such that Geertz's definition of culture, which we have already met, as 'the ensemble of narratives we tell ourselves about ourselves', is now dominated by television. It is so dominated not only by the mere fact of the hours spent watching it, but also by all it does to provide us with explanatory narratives which we use to enclose, understand and interpret, as best we can, ourselves and the news of the world.

The link between this large generalization and the present moment of culture which it encloses is the work of Stuart Hall. He anticipates much of what there is to say in chapter 6 about postmodernity and does so as having been Hoggart's lieutenant and then his successor at the Birmingham Centre for Contemporary Cultural Studies. Not only that: he came to England a black West Indian with a Rhodes Scholarship to Oxford and to read English literature; he came in the vanguard of those several thousands who followed from the Caribbean to find a better job and, they hoped, a welcoming society in what many in the early 1950s could still think of as the mother country.

When Hall addressed himself to culture, therefore, he was predisposed to find it political, for sure – he was himself, and not accidentally, one of the first thinkers to introduce Gramsci to anglophone academics – and, consequently, a site of fierce contestation. Marx provided him with a physics to explain the bitter class oppositions bombarding one another in culture (as did the ordinary battered life of the secondary modern schoolteacher Hall briefly was), and being a black colonial subject as well as a man of dazzling confidence and charm, striking intelligence, and unusually capacious feelings, he was predisposed to find culture as defined by the University not only 'a storehouse of recorded value' (the phrase is

Leavis's), but also a record telling of barbarism as well as civilization, cruelty along with nobility, shame alongside honour.

Hall's prodigal writings are almost all brief; they are a succession of new starts; the discarding of many, briefly attempted, new theorizations; the trying-out of provisional ideas; rapid sketches for the solution of local difficulties; all this in prose that can be, at different times feather light, jargon heavy, morally trenchant, irresistibly forgiving. What Hall's life's work does for our subject-matter is to swing us from the sufficiently settled cities of modernism, the cultures of national identity and political certainty confirmed by war and Cold War, to the placeless unfixity of the present. As much in his life as in his work, this grave, handsome, nice and sympathetic man alerts us to the 'new times'[30] in which culture is become 'a sensuous human praxis, the activity through which men and women make history'.[31] It is an activity in endless negotiation (a word with which he makes perhaps too much play), taking place in a world whose social orders endlessly seek domination, never more so than when under the command of capital. Yet in this diverse, differentiated, fragmentary life of culture one may discern 'new rhythms' fighting for life, caught between commercial deathliness and cultural vitality, and speaking 'words as material as the world'.[32]

This mixed quintet of men has taught us across sixty years the *reciprocity of narrative as being the physics of modern culture*. 'Britons make it, it makes Britons', the old Shredded Wheat cereal packets used proudly to say forty years ago. There is a theory of culture in the slogan, and if our culture is not yet synonymous with television, television is unmistakably the primary determinant of our leisure and consequently of that time we have which is our own and, as we cheerfully say, free. Perhaps it should be added that to criticize modern or any other culture is not necessarily to denounce it. The great strength and facility of what has, partly because of the work of the men compressed into this one chapter, become the discipline of Cultural Studies, is that it finds plenty of good things to live for.

5
The Social Production of Culture

I

When the first anthropologists started their work, the prevailing metaphors for social-theoretical use were largely those of nineteenth-century heavy engineering. Even today few words have a more compelling and immediate authority in the human sciences than 'structure' and, when Durkheim first launched the word into sociology before Evans-Pritchard and company took it up gratefully, it seems likely enough that they had in mind the structures of, say, bridges, big city buildings, tanks, railway engines – anything the building of which involved girders, plating, rivets, and massive lifting equipment, all to be assembled cumulatively, level piled on level, in the tremendous clamour of traditional industry.

Social structure, for all its 'factuality', was none the less (as Radcliffe-Brown said) a metaphor, but in theoretical discussion and above all in diagrams, it was grasped imaginatively as four-square and rising upwards level by level. The language of class (working, middle, upper) confirmed such a picture, which was in turn formalized by the regular publication of a national *Directory of Occupations* by the British government's Stationery Office. This classified all occupations as belonging to one of six levels, in which 'mental' workers all appeared at the top and 'manual' at the bottom, with the elderly and derelict counted out altogether and low-status clerical workers dividing category three (C) with high-status and more technically trained manual workers.

No doubt the hierarchies of information technology have complicated these distinctions, but stratification theory is still in active business. When the so-called structuralists had their shortish day in command of human science, their self-designation announced as thesis the discovery of stout and permanent structures as features of all social life. Indeed, Marxists discovered in their founding fathers, Marx and Engels, a model of society in which the economic base (down in the engine-room) drove the systems of production, while constructed on top of the base was a cultural superstructure corresponding to the mechanisms below but immobile without them.

At about the same time, Freud had devised his no less stratified model of every human psyche, in which superego, ego, and id competed for temporary mastery but in which the subconscious mind and its libido toyed with the conscious one and its sporadic efforts at reason and sublimation.

Structuralism, an intellectual movement of the 1960s and 1970s, took its sudden, terrific burst of energy from these ancestors, put its faith in the metaphor of structure but propounded its theories in a very different climate from that in which its great originators operated. Marx and Freud were attempting to found a science of society as hard and sure as the sciences of unreflective matter. The latter-day structuralists also made their call on the certitude of science, as Lévi-Strauss did in his ambition to describe a periodic table of the cultural elements. They were encouraged in this venture by the intervening success of theoretical linguistics and its discovery of non-temporal and structural constants in the unstoppable flow of language. Ferdinand de Saussure and Roman Jakobson gave their disciples the hope that all human activity was contained by dynamic forces with determinate forms. The intellectual problem was then to detect these invisibles in the stiff, three-dimensional regularities of human conduct, just as one may track electricity moving through a field of resistance.

Structuralism still thrives, although cocksureness has gone out of it. One way of explaining its loss of confidence would be to say that the nineteenth-century conception of culture turned out to be too mechanical and its hydraulics too generalizable to be a usable explanation. The structuralists were no less intent than their founders on formulating the laws – the observable and dependable regularities – of social life. One reason they lost their way was that they were unable to do so, but this disappointment coincided with that widespread critical movement which did so much to break up both hardline positivism (or the pursuit of fixed facts) in the human sciences and the view that human behaviour could be rendered as predictable as the laws of gravity and the movement of the heavens.

Those laws themselves, however, turned out to be more complex than some lawgivers had supposed, but, as one would expect, rarefied advances in physical science took a long time to affect the range of metaphors conventional in the human sciences. In any case, with the victory of anti-positivism and the petering-out of grand theoretical collaboration between the social sciences, human scientific enquiry had, as the history of anthropology suggests, taken 'the cultural turn',[1] that is, it had turned away from metaphors of framework, osteopathy, engineering, and three-dimensional modelling, to those of cartography, aesthetics, discourse theory, and Gestalt perspectivism. The ambition of the social science faculties at Harvard and Chicago during the 1950s had been to style themselves 'Departments of Social Relations' (Harvard), to found committees 'On Social Thought' or 'Ideas and Methods' (Chicago) and to send out their cleverest scholars on the roads 'Towards a Common Language for the Social Sciences'.[2] The assorted titles declared not only an allegiance to the then-new idea of interdisciplinarity but something larger, more American, more generous-hearted, and, as it turned out, thoroughly unworkable, which was a vision of the enlightened understanding of the texture of all social life accomplished by energetic synthesis of all the human sciences. This would be achieved by pooling everything human scientists produced: ethnographic data, statistics, economic surveys, theory grand and minor, questionnaire returns by the million, interviews and their schedules by the thousand, fieldwork reports of every kind.

Structure suffered setbacks, especially the ambition to provide general theories of the forms of social action which could be applied transculturally and in all human circumstances. It was, you might say, culture itself which put a stop to such optimistic vacuities. Human enquiry came up against two recalcitrant states of affairs, one conceptual but indissoluble, the other empirical and inalterable. In the first, the powerfully idealizing charge in culture, the deposits of human hopefulness in its concept, meant that cultural action was always liable to reflexive improvement. Theories implicit in culture as to how things might be better caused people to change conduct in response to theory. Belief itself, as visible in action of all kinds (from the making of art to the making of love), could be theoretically modified even as the theoretician was conducting his or her scientific observances.

The second, empirical difficulty was that culture signalled both difference and likeness, but in either manifestation would represent itself bifocally according to whether you interpret it through the lens of human solidarity or of cultural variety. Whichever you choose, the structure of the action cannot remain innate. It must be attributed by the observer; in which case, you may be better off abandoning claims to have identified, to use Talcott Parsons's famous title, *The Structure of Social Action*,[3] and settling instead for faithfully described recreations of culture in one dimension at a time, but given a less solitary perspective and a more resonant context by comparison.

This is one knotted-up crux at the heart of the matter of cultural enquiry. Inasmuch as it has been the discipline of sociology which has offered to provide a science of the social production of culture, it has been sociologists who, baffled by the knot in the crux, have retreated from it warily. Instead, they have taken permission from the meaning of culture-as-way-of-life to circumscribe social group or social activity within the safe limits of 'subculture', and treated the persons they had marked off as though they were as remote, exotic, and uninfluenced by elsewhere as the Trobriand Islanders or the Inuit.

Richard Hoggart's celebrated Birmingham Centre for Contemporary Cultural Studies took advantage of this intellectual easing of the theoretical problem and, admonished by both Marx and Hoggart's successor Stuart Hall, followed the subcultures of social formation in order to determine, for example, how working-class boys get working-class jobs,[4] and how – in a speculative and daring departure from those conventions which assumed the amiable harmlessness of culture – cultural practices may provide time and space not merely to subvert what rulers say by making faces at them, but rather instruct their members in the hard and put-upon disciplines of class resistance.

Even Birmingham's contribution was, however, a small eddy compared to the stream of now-neglected studies of working- and under-class ethnographies launched and propagated in the 1920s and 1930s by Robert Park at the University of Chicago. Not much cited nowadays, he was none the less a generative presence in the making of Chicago's powerful reputation in sociology and social enquiry in general, which culminated in the establishment of the university's more-or-less national and all-embracing committees on social thought and on ideas and methods mentioned earlier.

Those committees foundered on the blank impossibility of the task they set themselves, namely to pile absolutely everything into one theoretical transformer and turn the handle. It was Robert Park's genius intuitively to grasp the incommensurability of millions of items of individual data with the intersubjective life of cultural interaction.[5] Park saw – and this is the truth I intend to emphasize most in this book – the *irreducibility* of human interaction and its products as gathered under the heading of culture.

The German social theorists Georg Simmel and Edmund Husserl coined the adjective 'intersubjective' to affirm this truth. Park had read Simmel on 'The Philosophy of Money', and (Simmel's most famous essay) 'The Stranger in the Metropolis', but he had also, after leaving Harvard in 1899, been press agent for the great black activist, Booker T. Washington, and had earlier spent ten years first as a reporting journalist and then as an editor. He learned about the philosophy of money and the terrors and thrills of the metropolis in the two most frightening and thrilling cities in the world, New York and Chicago. When, aged fifty, he became a professor of sociology, he was in a position to teach his subject plenty about the elusive omnipresence of culture and the challenge of finding its factuality not in questionnaires or standardized interviews, nor in the mindlessness of box-formula content analysis, but in the canons of 'empathy and distance' acquired from journalism.

The phrase was Park's own, but it proved no licence for a soft-hearted lack of method. Park took more than metaphors from the new sciences of medical cartography and environmental context. He mapped an epidemiology of cultural phenomena, marking the zones of the city in which they flourished ('moral regions')[6] and, borrowing from ecological theory the concepts of invasion and succession, theorized the culture of cities as a Darwinian struggle for the preservation of species (classes, ethnicities, professions, social activities) in which the key achievement is marking out and winning space.

Given his life's work up to the age of fifty, it was natural for him to observe moderately, 'One might fairly say that a sociologist is merely a more accurate, responsible and scientific reporter'[7] (Max Weber said almost exactly the same thing a few years earlier).[8] The observation is paid for by experience. As I have consistently emphasized, the history of a concept is the history of its *use* – its use, that is, as an instrument of thought by men and women battling to make sense of life by ascribing explanations to its mystery. Hence the glimpses of individual biography with which I hint at the living experiences, predicaments and disputes from which culture took the meanings it has.

The very titles of the books published by the Chicago School as inspired by Park indicate the enlargement of the definitions of culture which he gave sociology first, and the conversation of culture itself as a consequence: Norman Hayner's *The Sociology of Hotel Life*, classics such as Harvey Zorbaugh's *The Gold Coast and the Slum* (about New York), Ernest Shideler's *The Chain Store*, Helen MacGill Hughes's *News and the Human Interest Story*, and – still easily available for everyday perusal – Nels Anderson's *The Hobo*, Frederic Thrasher's *The Gang*, Louis Wirth's *The Ghetto*. This little shower of namedrops may help shimmer the honoured name of Chicago sociology, as is only right. Conceptual history is also a matter of paying proper tribute. Its urgency in the period covered by this chapter, however, is evidence of the thickness and high density that the concept of culture was accumulating by this time, and its utter lack of amenability to conventional sociological quantification. Park and his followers cut their concept a dozen ways in terms of groups of solitaries, of neighbourhoods, of value, time and space, and of the sumptuous comedy of commonplace institutions. They were reporters, anecdotalists, ethnographers, keepers of urban myths, explicators of a society to itself.

There is still a tension, however, between those whose work embodies an anti-theoretical cast of mind, who prefer principles to theory, interpretation to explanation, and reasons to causes, as opposed to those who hanker after the success and certitude of traditionally scientific kinds of finality. This is not a fight to be fixed between warm old humanists and cold hard scientists. It is a coexistence and a struggle between individual insight and grand-theoretical narrative. The rest of this chapter will seek ecumenically to dispense prizes to both.

II

In this brief history of the varieties of cultural method, we may say that the English remained true enough to their Anglo-Saxon habits of empiricism and faithfulness to the facts, while the Americans veered between plans for a corporate empire of quantifaction, far more easygoing routines of not unkindly surveillance, and the strenuous search for durable metaphors with which to accommodate copious fieldwork. The Cartesian French, on the other hand, are still pledged to method and the Parisian Marxism of the *grandes écoles*, the rigorous logic and absolutes of the Enlightenment *philosophes*. Nor is this a reproach. Intellectual enquiry and the morality of method have been, if not globalized, then radically Europeanized these past fifty years. The mind of the French has had mesmerizing effects on all sides, as the success and hysterics of deconstruction prove.

It is of course the paradox of deconstruction that it instructs its followers with such undeviating sternness in hyper-scepticism. The French logical style extends even to the illogic of the subconscious ('The subconscious,' declared Lacan immortally, 'is structured like a language.') But two of the greatest French champions of structure and its reality in social action stick to the idea less wilfully and are sure that only with its help can order be asserted over the protean and glutinous subjects and objects of culture.

The objects of their enquiry are typically French – French tragic drama of the seventeenth century in the first case, the French uses of culture within class structure, together with Algerian cultural defences against the depredations of capital in the second. Both men, Lucien Goldmann and Pierre Bourdieu,[9] were crucially influenced by Marxism in the institutionalized form in which Marxism is taught and inherited at the Collège de France. They were also soaked in the inheritance of Emile Durkheim. Durkheim was much divided between his strong acquiescence in the nineteenth century's determination to make human science a truly natural science, and his deep feeling for the irreducibly interactive nature of the instinctive creativity which makes the human world. On the one hand, he wrote his didactic primer, *The Rules of Sociological Method*, to teach his disciples how to spot a social fact; on the other, he identified the impalpability of what he was the first to call the *conscience collective*,[10] that unstoppable social collusion which makes every private individual an involuntary product of what we may as well call the public realm of culture. Durkheim set his heirs the impossible task of recovering from inside the germinations and flowering of collective consciousness the determinant structures which ordered its growth.

I suppose one could say that the aspiration was to build a molecular biology of culture. Lucien Goldmann called it 'genetic structuralism' and set himself to connect structures to selves, and to find a way of recovering the context of creation without dissolving the cultural texts into it. His ambition was to keep faith, certainly, with Marxism's historical materialism and the contortions of class struggle in the systems of production, but to replace the crude Marxist image of culture as merely a mirror of production, in order to analyse what had actually been done by cultural producers and their collective consciousness to acknowledge or reconcile the contradictions of history. He intended to dissect the new shoots of green culture and trace the path of their mutations.

Goldmann, none the less, remains attached to the traditional categories of aesthetics. Culture retains its idealizing element even while each product registers the profane distortions of class. So Goldmann turns to the French seventeenth century and the writings, more monumental than canonical for any Frenchman of his intellectual formation in *lycée* and *grande école*, of Blaise Pascal and Jean Racine.

Both writers were members of the *noblesse de robe*, the class of courtiers who had sworn unquestioning fealty to Louis XIV, the Sun King, but who now found themselves cut off from the royal presence and the domestic intimacies which they gratefully performed as signs of a servitude that was for them synonymous with perfect freedom. The monarch, it appears, had severed their dependency as part of a crafty series of political innovations designed to provide himself with a much-needed and modernizing bureaucracy as France joined the long revolution of the European powers towards the modern state.

But the very identity of the *noblesse de robe* – its moral horizon and the definition of its social role – was built around their personal subjection to the throne, and the self-abasing rituals which its members performed around it. They were caught by a huge historical shift in social structure: the advent of the new class of professional administrators, the displacement of antique feudalism by a half-way modernizing absolutism,[11] the beginnings of the end of spectacular display as the means of rule.

In Goldmann's compelling, thick-textured but conclusively simple analysis, Pascal and Racine wrote, respectively, the philosophy and the tragic drama which expressed the insoluble predicament of their class. Goldmann had been much impressed by the lead given in theorizing culture by the great Hungarian critic of politics-in-culture, Georg Lukács, who had surmised[12] that, to become effective on the stage of history, social classes have to come to a consciousness of themselves and their potential as actors on that stage. He stipulated certain criteria as needing to be present before a class had attained the kind of maturity and progressivism he was talking about and, in a separate essay,[13] observed in passing that Mozart's music perfectly fulfilled the implicit messages of the German Enlightenment as combining reason and happiness. Mozart unites order and passion with such ravishing sweetness that his music opens at its centre into an invitation to a rational happiness which, it seems, prefigures the dance of the good society.

Goldmann carried Lukács's speculations off into the darker territory of the Jansenist girls' school for whom Racine wrote his later tragedies. The Jansenists taught unquestioning obedience to an awful godhead whose forgiveness was arbitrary and for whom the gift of grace had nothing to do with good works. Catholics they certainly were, but their view of the justice of God's punishment upon irredeemable humanity was comparable to that of the heretical Jean Calvin of Geneva.

It was a theology, Goldmann noticed, which exactly fitted (and was inseparable from) the politics of the *noblesse de robe*. In both, passion was exaction and duty a commandment. So when Racine wrote his greatest tragedy, *Phèdre*, for the schoolgirls, the small space of its chamber-drama contained a world-view reflecting the gaze of God.

The tale comes from Ancient Greek myth, the only source of non-Christian narrative permitted the virgin scholars. Phèdre, second wife of the widowed king, falls terribly in love with her stepson, Hippolite. She is ripped emotionally apart by the hideousness of incest pulling against the torrents of desire. Loss (and sex) is a monster; the best-known line in the play is 'C'est Vénus tout entière à sa proie attachée': Venus is a dreadful bird with her razor beak sunk in her prey. Like the *noblesse de robe* in their extremity, Phèdre plays out her passion in a series of long speeches made to a confidante as powerless as she is herself. Hippolite, the object of unsated, insatiable desire, is horribly dismembered by a supernatural bull sea-shouldering its way up from the Mediterranean, disgorged from some pre-theistic slumber by Phèdre's helpless violation of nature and culture.

Goldmann presents this savage and serene tale, told to one another by the protagonists and their personal servants in a tempest of self-contained anguish, as Racine's extended metaphor, dramatizing, intensifying, and enshrining as visible the plight of his class. The sociology of culture here permits us to recognize how the genius of the poet must needs work not just with the events of public life, but as he is worked upon by their deep unapprehended structure. The hope is, then, that the sociologist, like the anthropologist, can explain the 'reconstituted totality', anachronistically but none the less in terms that Racine himself could in principle have grasped.

III

The historical sociology of culture cannot be told apart from cultural history itself. The sociology of contemporary culture is caught in a different bind. Here, the offer to explain ourselves to ourselves is up against our assumption that we know what's going on already. Pierre Bourdieu's first theoretical sally was in fact into the decidedly untheoretical war of liberation in Algeria.

Bourdieu had been brought up in Gascony, son of a poor, independent market-gardener-peasant who doubled as village postman, crossed the Mediterranean and committed himself early to the new kind of anthropology welcomed in the third chapter, in which the subject is not the study of circumscribable exotics, but the clash of modern and traditional societies, one senior and exploitative, the other junior and oppressed, both inextricably entangled with each other over a long history. He set himself to understand what was happening to what he called 'the subproletarians' and might now be called the underclass. These were the landless, unskilled, mostly unemployed Muslim Arab men whose traditional pieties and definitions of gain, trust, honour, and livelihood were all disintegrating under the generalized impact of capitalism as it crossed the Mediterranean a few years after the end of World War Two ignited their Civil War.

Bourdieu was intent on giving his sociology a dynamic edge. In the routine sleepwalking of simple-minded Marxism nobody has any freedom of action because the ultimate determinant power is rooted in the systems of production. Ordinary solidarity with his Algerians made Bourdieu feel this theory of passivity to be merely insolent, and in any case unsatisfactory as to the facts of life. Marxism, put at its most general, makes the collective the paramount entity in social movement. Liberalism, also by definition, sets the voluntary individual as the realm and fount of social energy. Bourdieu sought a convincing explanation of individuals' resistance to the determinants of economic systems. He sought to realize Durkheim's ambitions.

He came up with his most famous single concept, the 'habitus'. 'The habitus,' he says, 'is a system of durable, transposable dispositions which functions as the generative basis of structured, objectively unified practices.'[14] Expressed in this rather cumbersome tautology, it isn't much help. The trick is to find it, with all the subtlety this calls for, systematically at work in ostensive action.

Bourdieu proceeds to this, armed with the friendly if rather general premiss that capitalism is an undifferentiated, pervasive, colossal, and malignant force. What it does it does to the detriment of traditional Arab society, particularly this very poor corner of it. Bourdieu aims to discover the form and force of those 'customary dispositions' which have outlasted most of the economic base of their formation, and to see, angrily, compassionately, and in the diction of objectivity, how 'some remnants of the pre-capitalist mode of production persist despite everything, *and with them*, the associated dispositions'.[15]

This is what it is to live residual values, and Bourdieu took as the realm in which the discrepancy between antique-residual and dominant-oppressive values is most stark the ways Algerian peasants tell the time and square time against money. He is left with bitter truths about what capitalism has done to the traditional ways there are for these poor to protract debts, never to make ends meet but to keep the gap bearable, to hold each one of them in the body of society.

'Ethos is carried straight through into ethics'[16] in the old ways; but then, as Bourdieu does not say, so it is in capitalism. Disposition – the habitus – is created by ethos, and ethos, we may say, is almost a synonym for culture, as long as you think both terms connote a structure. In the old ways, however, 'wastage of time . . . and wastage of means are perhaps the condition of survival of societies which, if they counted, would give up'.[17] That they never give up is why Bourdieu admires their desperate tenacity and why he sings his lament to their slow, painful defeat.

The pain of his sympathy brings Bourdieu to a formulation of his difficulties with culture expressed in the severe idiom of French human-scientific duty. 'The anthropologist has the task of reconstituting the totality from which it is possible to discover the unity between subjective experience, a distorted apprehension of the social system, and the objective structure which scientific reflection constructs or discovers.'[17]

Human scientific understanding reconstitutes in an inclusive whole the feelingful life of the wretched Arabs, their sense, inevitably distorted, of their place and meaning in social life, and the *structural* account of all this which the scientist can best put together ('constructs' or 'discovers', in Bourdieu's own verbs). No one element is privileged over the other. Only the 'reconstituted totality' provides the final exposition, the explanatory narrative, of ragged men with etched skin and broken teeth, grinning embarrassedly on the market's edge as they share a tiny pot of coffee.[18]

The Algerians Bourdieu encountered in 1960 now know a great deal more about the impact of capitalism and are well able to put together the nuts and bolts of home-made theory. So the sociologist has to work a new magic. In a new venture, Bourdieu therefore set himself to uncover the dynamic structure which drove moral evaluations deep into those 'durable, transposable dispositions' that we have already encountered. He was in pursuit of those tendencies of the habitus which may be quickened into new forms of action, thereby altering the shape of 'civil affections'.

The field of his study was to be art itself, and hence of culture as it aspired to this ideal. Its exact location in the field (he pioneered the borrowing of field-theory from particle physics and putting it to work in the human sciences) was to be at the point of collision between class taste and the strict, implicit rules of art dictated by society for the observation of artists.[19] Bourdieu's general heading for this examination was 'reproduction theory': how do cultural practices and their concomitant dispositions become intertwined and made durable and continuous? Where personal taste is at stake, everyone gets touchy.

What have come to be called the 'meaning industries' are responsible in all industrial societies for the production of culture, the political economy of symbolic goods. They organize the production, circulation and reproduction of social meaning by means of the cultural system: the industries comprise the institutions of publication and broadcasting (the mass media and public communicators), of education and storage (schools, libraries, universities, tape companies, the underclass of keyboard-operators), of primary production (writers, artists, photographers, film and TV directors, and so forth, with the same underclass).

Bourdieu begins from two truisms about the cultural industries and the relations of production which form them. These are the class divisions which are the generators of competitiveness within the industries; the first is classically between the dominant and dominated classes; the second is found within the dominant class itself, and divides its dominated and dominant fractions. Bourdieu writes: 'At the deepest level of the class ethos, the dominated class rejects the dominant culture in a movement of pure negation.'[20] It is this convulsion of rejection with which schoolteachers are so familiar and which liberalism must partly deny, partly compromise with.

The dominant fraction controls material reproduction in the sphere of production (the serious money), its dominated or subaltern fraction is assigned to the legitimation of material reproduction (money, again, and power) through the exercise of symbolic power (cultural rewards, the power given to those who are educated and cultivated). This summary gives rise to an austere axiom. 'Intellectuals . . . will always struggle to maximise the autonomy of the cultural field and to raise the social value of the specific competences . . . by raising the scarcity of those competences.'[21] More compactly, we may say that the intelligentsia keeps its distinctiveness by making its subject difficult to do. Amongst the employees of the meaning industry (or as Bourdieu has it, within the dominated fraction of the dominant class, whose concern is with the exercise of symbolic power), there are different groups struggling for dominance within their corner of the division of labour, the allotments in the fields of their subject. Such and such are the competitions within the rules of which thinkers must try to tell their particular truths.

In a bold move, Bourdieu extends the concept of capital itself to culture. He asserts as a premiss that those who hold cultural capital use it as they would economic capital: they invest it, accumulate it, live off its interest, inherit it, lose it in doomed enterprises, seek out new products and fields of exploitation, subject it to the systems of mass production – in short, they compete with it.

'Cultural capital' as a term covers all the knowledge of the key cultural topics which a person has by virtue of inheritance and formal education; it could include informal learning acquired from one's family and the common knowledge of a social class, as well as the diplomas, certificates, degrees, and doctorates from official schooling and of varying status. In all this accumulation (and loss), hoarding and extravagance, however, the secret of this cultural currency is that it holds its value only by being counterposed to economic circulation. This is Bourdieu's maxim. For the sake of its own autonomy and its sharp distinction from the economic (that is, wealthy) fraction of the bourgeoisie, the cultural fraction (which in the end has to concede dominance to the economic fraction), must deny the primacy of capital and affirm that of culture. The rich, as Hemingway said to Scott Fitzgerald, have more money; the cultivated, therefore, must ensure the special value – the Distinction, as Bourdieu's title has it – of its culture.

Thus, rather than cashing in cultural for economic capital, the cultural capitalist translates his symbolism from wealth and comfort into rarity and cultural purity, distinction indeed. This transference is prepared for during the period of accumulation of cultural capital (by piling up three university degrees) and by the exigence and self-denial demanded as payment for this accumulation: the doctoral student earns very little money.

In the cut-throat competition of contemporary capitalism, investments in culture – art, wine, antiques, food, architecture, travel – are brutally subordinated to the new technologies of money. Financial analysts, investment bankers, and their software stooges have the old guardians of high symbolism on the run. Holders of symbolic capital are in thrall to real capital as never before.

Desperately seeking to maintain competitive standing *vis-à-vis* far more powerful opponents in the realm of economic capital, the cultural capitalist must nevertheless strive for a superior level of cultural competence, consumption and accumulation. This competence turns on his or her power to bestow and consecrate value, which is then socially ratified. Again, in Bourdieu's axiom, disavowal of the economic is the governing principle upholding the maintenance of the value of cultural capital. However much the artist or intellectual may desire money at a personal level, and say so, the production of culture under capitalism is only possible within a value-system which, while endorsing cultural practices that 'deny the economic', none the less stands in crucial relation to that economy.

Thus, the cultural capitalist keeps up the high level of his competence by justifying his distinction as culturally and not economically acquired. Consequently, it cannot be a class distinction, although keeping its value high requires such class necessities as sufficient time, space, and money, as well as such currencies as command discourse. Whatever its political or moral orientation (left or right, young or old, black or white, male or female), Bourdieu contends that the iron rules of the social field will hold, and the habitus of culture – its principles of regulation and transformation – not only accommodates, it demands the conflicts of competition. In order to keep their balance, the cultural capitalists must play off the cultural against the economic, and are trapped within their class's constituent fractions, as between the dominant and the emergent, the endless competition of the generations.[22] Thus, schools of cultural production typically compete using claims about their validity over those of other schools, and each school has to maintain this competition by demonstrating (to its credit) its own allegiance to the laws of the field. This credit is in turn validated as more authentic, more pure-mindedly faithful to the one tradition and its originary values. Only in this way can the new generation intending revaluation supplant the old. In Bourdieu, the inevitability of this process gives rise to a further axiom: 'As judges we reproduce in the space of the judgements whereby we classify work and self the space within which we are ourselves classified. *The only escape from this perfect circle is to objectify it.*'[23]

There is an exact and visible correspondence between the competing groups in the market-place and the fractions of the subaltern class who staff the cultural industries. The two segments of cultural and economic capital sit in a structural complementarity. Within it, each segment rationally and honestly defends its mutual interests against its competitors in material production.

IV

It is by way of these mechanisms that intellectual élites gain their advantages, and these same frictions drive the production of culture in those giant industries which now dominate its manufacture, pricing, circulation, and obsolescence. Every new producer must seek to displace rivals by (in Bourdieu's powerful phrase) 'producing time' itself; must, therefore, so display the key cultural values of innovation and originality that rivals are supplanted because of their out-of-dateness. Senior producers, on the other hand, must seek to hold their position by virtue of their product reliability. Thus, the radical innovator finds support and audience in the future; the conservative of the present must find coevals in the past, and an audience which would rather purchase reassurance and recognition than disturbance and revelation.

Bourdieu's sociology steers, as it is bound to do, between one classical function of such enquiry, which is to tell the unaccommodating truths masked by the social conventions and to try to prove them by counting up the facts of life, and the other, which is to determine the rules (rather than the laws) of social engagement. His larger ambition is to discover a sociology capable of articulating the two in a single explanatory algebra. If such a device were to be invented, it would then be capable of unlocking certain life-secrets; it would enclose the bombarding energies of status-acquisition within the strong but flexible structures which order the patterns not only of social organization but also of social being. It would, as Bourdieu does, dispute and analyse taste in culture, which is no less than the seat of judgement and the realm of our most distinctive allegiances. Any such activity puts everyone's self-justification and self-esteem at risk, including that of the sociologist (as Bourdieu points out).[24] For the origin of taste lies in class, and class is allocated by education and by the accumulations of capital, cultural or economic.

This is less blank than it sounds. The extraordinary data-collecting labours which support Bourdieu's theories in *Distinction* and his other relevant works[25] can be read with the fascination of Balzac or Proust. The wounds of class, as his research team reported, of museum- and art-gallery-goers, are so immediately and painfully familiar. These signs are, as Bourdieu tells us, 'a reminder of the social conditions and conditioning which made [them] possible . . . both an obvious fact and an outrage'. As they always do, however, 'the privileged classes of bourgeois society replace the difference between two cultures, products of history reproduced by education, with the basic difference between two natures, one nature naturally cultivated, and another nature naturally natural'.[26]

That this is so does no damage at all to the necessity we all feel, never more than in our dealing with culture, to make what Charles Taylor calls our 'strong evaluations', our 'distinctions of worth',[27] what an older tradition of cultural commentary called simply 'our value-judgements'. Taylor's view – it is one upheld by the most cursory reading of the past two or three thousand years of literature and philosophy – is that these strong evaluations are what give life meanings and persons characters. When sociology unmasks our pretensions and anthropology dissolves our categories, neither kind of logic threatens our determination to figure out the good and to prefer the truth. Each aims rather to remove the obstacles to seeing the truth, and to open the way to finding the good.

These are shy-making terms these days. What kind of human scientist would now dare to identify the mysteries of culture which direct social actors towards virtue? But I do not doubt that the *point* of theorizing culture is to consider what form of life may conduce to well-being and human flourishing, and those other forms, themselves so obviously flourishing at the present time, which conduce to shaping lives in the images of the pig and the rat.

The intellectual conundrum is to illuminate how culture fires up our being either unattractive creatures, or something more lovable; how, in the technical jargon, structure crunches up agency; how, in everyday language, we each of us match decisions about what to do and pictures of who we are to behaviour which makes sense and conduct which expresses life. Bourdieu, fascinated by this difficulty, carried it off to the plane of theoretical abstraction, where the habitus spontaneously fastens together disposition and cultural form, each modifying the other in the encounter. Geertz, never one for grand theory, finds culture in action – in the cockfight, in the heated meetings of local government,[28] in the familiar items of anthropological enquiry – beliefs, rituals, customs, dramas. Describing the action, discovering its multiple narratives, for actors (them) and for audience (us), *is the same thing* as finding the key values of a society (dominant, residual, emergent) arranged and made visible as the constellations of its culture.

V

Searching for the intellectual virtues, and in hot pursuit of the game of culture, anthropology has always been best at spotting passion in action, sociology at fixing the determinants of order. One British sociologist, working alone in the tradition of Anglo-Saxon empiricism but with his own keen sense of the impossible ambiguities of meaning which crowd round the facts, came – for my money at least – nearest of all to catching culture at just the moment it turned into character.

Basil Bernstein, who died in 2001 at the age of seventy-five, started out in the 1960s from the then-prevalent mixture of British sociological realism and a simple-minded theory of social-cultural correspondence inherited from Durkheim, which reasonably assumed that cultural behaviour directly reflected social structure. Bernstein, working-class child of a Jewish mother converted to Catholicism, an early school-leaver brought obliquely to university education by way of wartime service in flying-boats, was perhaps the first sociologist after Durkheim to discover the informal traces of culture in the formal systems of school knowledge.

In those days, the fledgling sociology of culture was still tied to the protocols of science. You shaped a hypothesis and tested it experimentally. Bernstein chose two groups of small children, one working class, one middle (the categories were clearer then), and asked them to describe the story they saw in a series of illustrations. The results, now famous or infamous according to your political preferences and readiness to take offence, suggested to him that working-class children told their stories in terms restricted to their immediate interlocutors, contextualized by reference to gestures ('look, here, this'), specific as to demonstratives (using, therefore, pronouns rather than nouns), terse as to syntax, matter-of-fact rather than speculative. The middle-class children, by obliging contrast, generalized their account beyond their listener, broke free from context, elaborated the available narrative (using nouns not pronouns) in sentences supported by relative clauses, and proceeded from description to explanation.

These cognitive habits, Bernstein surmised, were learned in the respective cultural habitats of the children. For the working-class group, these were close, crowded, verbally thrifty, bound by immediate circumstance and distant apprehension; for the middle class, cognitive life was tied less to its neighbourhood, emphasized the distinctiveness of individuality, encouraged verbal extravagance, and anticipated the freedoms of the future.

The moral of all that, as Bernstein put it later in a trenchant essay with the same title, was that 'education cannot compensate for society',[29] which was to say that the informal modes of cognitive-cultural life in the middle classes suited those who learned them early a good deal better for the demands of formal education than it did city-centre children. What one might do about this turned on one's political allegiances (which were for Bernstein himself emphatically egalitarian), but the decisive step was towards an identification of the genes of culture in the bloodshed of class struggle.

The identification was, however, in terms of culture as an undistorted reflection of social structure. Bernstein wanted to move closer to the point at which one became the other in a rhythm of continuous reciprocity. So he turned to the forms of educational knowledge, which is the readiest official definition and embodiment of a society's culture, and, in a brilliant *coup*, stopped the rhythm of reciprocity at the moment (in his terminology) at which 'classification' intersected with 'framing'.[30]

'Classification' means what it says: the system and its rationale, whereby a section of educational knowledge defines its characteristic concepts, its zones and boundaries of interest, its prevailing vocabulary and idiom, its typical intellectual geography, and its traditional history. 'Framing' signifies the way in which the relevant section of knowledge (possibly but not necessarily a subject-discipline) controls the method of its application, legislates its pedagogy, certificates its pupils, and marks out the course of its transmission.

With so delicate a device, it is somewhat brutal for me to translate 'classification' into curriculum and 'framing' into teaching method, but if we do so, and mark each, as Bernstein recommends, as 'strong' or 'weak', then the usefulness of this heuristic fairly jumps out at us. For strength in both aspects of knowledge (the didactic teacher with the rigid syllabus) makes for a secure identity, confident direction, narrow specialism, intellectual obedience. Weakness in both aspects, on the other hand, makes for porousness of identity, interdisciplinarity of reference, indecisiveness of method and either exploratory insouciance or bewilderment in the choice of subject-matter.

Once one has these two ideal types marked out, it is easy to fill in the space between them: weak classification with strong framing makes a student too much in thrall to method and methodist; the reverse turns him or her into a scavenger of library or laboratory, knowing what to do but not how to do it.

The march of Bernstein's thought since that classic paper over thirty years ago has been, as I would want to put it for the purposes of this book, towards the founding of a true discipline of cultural enquiry, which we may as well call Cultural Studies, notwithstanding the terrible tripe which has been written under that head. Bernstein, no doubt, aspires to grand theory, but not imperially so. He was simply one of the first thinkers to grasp that a quite new kind of society impended, one absolutely grounded and configured upon the dispositions, allocations and formalizations of different kinds of knowledge. This did not mean that older absolutes of possession – capital, land, dynasty – were discounted, only that everything would be hereafter filtered through the grids of knowledge, and the management of ignorance with its infinite caste-system would become the paramount instrument of the polity, would assign power and dependence, development and backwardness, success and failure.

Bernstein pursued his venture deep into what he called 'the pedagogic device',[31] and its efficient demarcation between those thoughts never before thought and hitherto unthinkable, and the processes of differentiation, allocation, and all the rest which turned strange thought into the familiarities of curricula, tagging them for difficulty or facility, for type of science (human or natural), for school or university, for the distinction between 'pure' or 'applied', for suitability as to gender (hard science for boys, soft humanism for girls), for danger (politics) or safety (literature), for triviality (television, sport), for relevance (business, economics). All this colossal edifice, so natural and taken for granted that one was not even aware that it had so partisan an architecture but assumed one's freedoms of the city of reason where everyone is welcome, is then subjected to Bourdieu's rules of competition and superannuation, the two sociologies coming together to shape the key to all contemporary mythologies.

For, as Bernstein realized, he had contrived a model of *all* of a society's knowledge, whether educated or customary, learned in classroom or kitchen, and, by distinguishing between its practical or its theoretical orientation, could codify its position in relation to all other such forms.[32] Theoretical knowledge mounts vertically towards the theory itself, practical knowledge (as in the commonplace business of everyday life) neither needs nor seeks theorization, but occupies sealed and horizontal adjacencies, awaiting the moment to be useful ('How do I replace a washer on a tap?' 'What is the way to the station?').

Such a grid is capable of extension to all the cognitive activities of a society. I now aim to show that cognition, or the motions of thought, and the passions inseparable from it, are shaped to its very bottom by culture.

VI

Ever since Descartes spoke his discourse on method in the seventeenth century, it has been habitual for the two-part rationalists still in charge of the human sciences to suppose that insofar as understanding is cool, detached and objective, then it is rational and commendable. Of course, the Romantic movement blew a great hole in the ideal picture of judicious reasoning, and David Hume himself tamped the explosive when, in his *Treatise on Human Nature*, he addressed the zenith of Enlightenment by saying, 'Reason is, and ought always to be, the slave of the passions'.

This was not to say, one should not have to say but does, that the primacy of passion runs away with reason in a Dionysian frenzy. Passion may be serene, laconic, clipped, cool, just as much as abandoned or aflame. Hume, indeed, swore good citizens to the cultivation of 'the civil affections', to which, once we are educated in them, he consigned his trust and the future of 'the decent society'.[33] A couple of hundred years later, Richard Rorty did much the same, when he reckoned to have dispatched to the dustbin of history the idea that nature may be perfectly rendered to us in the lucid reflection of a perfect science, and preferred instead a sympathetic understanding of the human predicament by way of its gradual edification and a careful induction into the principles of moral-sympathetic interpretation.[34]

The concern of this section is, therefore, to find a sufficient convergence between the austerities of more-or-less structuralist accounts of the production of culture and this acknowledgement that in the human sciences the human passions are at once movers and moved, subjects and objects of enquiry, whichever takes precedence in a sentence, and depending on whether the speaker is participant or observer. That this is so in a culture in which culture is by now almost synonymous with visual narratives is one measure of how late it is to put the passions at the centre of our long-awaited 'science of human affairs'.

To do this, we shall return to Raymond Williams and his theoretical invention, 'the structure of feeling'. Williams tinkered with this idea all his life and brought it, on occasions, to unusually detailed if formidably abstract formulation. As he well knew, it was much easier to model social structures than to define the movement and purpose of barely articulated tremblings of feelings seeking expression. In an early cogitation on the usefulness of the term, he wrote of its elusiveness in

> a particular sense of life, a particular community of experience hardly needing expression, through which the characteristics of our way of life are in some way passed, giving them a particular and characteristic colour . . . a particular and native style . . . it is as firm as 'structure' suggests yet it operates in the most delicate and least tangible parts of our activity.[35]

Culture reappears as 'a way of life' but here animated by its passage through this 'particular sense' of what that life is. If we are to ally this apprehension of such dim presences to Geertz's 'constellation of enshrined ideas' we will clearly need some very refined habits of imaginative sympathy and moral sensibility. The big, no-nonsense words of social theory – words (and the blurry concepts they convey) like ideology, hegemony, complex formation, determinant, causality, and so forth – will hardly catch feelings in action.

One might object to Williams's endeavour that, although one recognizes at once what he is after, it is too impalpable to be caught and analysed. But this will not do. Such objections are always made to difficult new concepts (for example, to Kant's 'noumen', Milton's 'liberty', Marx's 'class struggle'). This is the brutish turn of old Reaction, blocking emancipatory thought wherever it declares itself. Williams was endeavouring to keep faith with the first most important meanings carried by culture: its encouragement to the best a society may make of itself, its significance as a flag of hope. In a later revision of the idea, he wrote: 'The idea of a structure of feeling can be specifically related to the evidence of forms and conventions – semantic figures – which, in art and literature, are often among the very first indications that such a new structure is forming.'[36] Tiny variations in form and convention betray the presence of new frames of feeling, just as do variations in social manners or inflections in ritual. But for Williams, and for me, art is the prime necessity for the task in hand, and the locale in which one finds the first and most vivacious signs of imaginative reorganization and creative energy. It is worth adding that this may be no less apparent and compelling when the creative artist picks up the forms and conventions in order to restore to them older, now residual forces. In such circumstances, the cultural expression in question may seem at first sight conservative in form. Closer looking or listening then discovers that the old has been reconfigured in the new, that familiar patterns of order and convention have been quietly recast in such a way that old values glow in the refreshment of novelty.

The damnable thing about the art of modernism – and the expectations of an unprecedentedly fashion-conscious culture, come to that – is that it supposes that change is preferable to continuity and synonymous with novelty. The drastic ruptures with the past effected by the titans of modern art in the early twentieth century – T. S. Eliot, James Joyce, Pablo Picasso, Igor Stravinsky – created a climate in which culture was expected to renew itself in surges of revolutionary innovation. Revolution was much in the air in the 1920s and, as we have seen, culture and politics blended together in their hot appeal to a radical future.

That future may, however, emerge only from the past. After the revolutionary promises of Stalinism and Fascism, as well as those which continue to be made and broken by global capitalism, it might seem sensibly cautious to ask of creativity in culture, that it glory in the hope that life may be replenished and paradise on earth reimagined. At the same time, let us pray that it do so with a keen sense of the localism of things and of their comely domesticity.

These are not the words which usually feature in the idiom and characteristic style of secular academic disciplines. Academic life in most languages teaches habitual superciliousness, instinctive derogation, amazement at other people's naivety, penury of response, ungenerosity in acknowledgement. After Williams's powerful, muffled but moving appeals to the incipience of feelings as the touchstone of culture, it is timely to suggest what it would take to follow his injunctions. Culture entails our ardent aspirations towards the ideal of a realizably good society just as much as it does our keen and sympathetic engagement with the awfulness and tedium, along with the magnificence, of ways of life or social practices or whatever else you want to call the daily round of things.

Something quite so high-minded, common as it is to so many of our preceptors in the history of the idea of culture, has a somewhat embarrassing ring these days. And yet, as is made resonant by the authorities cited and admired at the end of my last chapter, hearing the appeal to the best that is in us – eager, bright, tender and resolute – is the point of the human sciences. The study of human being is scientific, for sure; but science is incorrigibly connected to human interests,[37] and humans are interested, as I said, not only in how things are but also in how they might be better. It is Williams's contention, and mine, that such interest, and the understanding it seeks, is best sustained by the highly self-conscious practice of matching a discerned structure of feeling to a felt one.

Feelings are inseparable from cognition and action; both impel the necessary human act of interpretation. Every act of interpretation is also an act of judgement. This is as true for the human agents who are the objects of our sociology as it is for the sociologists. Either way, the difficulty and the delight is always to distinguish, capture, and articulate the 'structure-in-agency', as the jargon has it. In other words, understanding on the part of the actor or the observer is both impelled and comprehended by a frame of feeling, and, as the metaphor of a 'frame' brings out, the constituent feelings enclose the action; give it shape and direction; place it in an intelligible sequence. They plot it. Feelings must have subjects, and the experience of feelings a structure. (Fear, for instance, is fear of something which is necessarily part of that structure, and in response to which the emotion is suitable. Nameless fear is therefore a neurotic condition.)

These subjects are given form by what Charles Taylor calls 'imports'.[38] Saying what a feeling is like is a matter of describing imports. Thus, in order to identify the structure of the feeling of shame, we identify the shameful features of the situation. This descriptive process is the start of the so-called hermeneutic (or interpretative) arc; it is completed as a circle when the features of the situation corroborate the feeling. Shame is then the right feeling to have. The feeling is our way of grasping 'imports', and entails an ethical component.

As we all know painfully, our first feeling will not be our last, and may be insufficient to the occasion. Feelings may be at odds with knowledge. Nonetheless, it seems reasonable to propose that the more a circumstance is absorbed by as full a play of all our best feelings (that is, adequate and relevant to the case), the more the import will be grasped and understood. Love, in the sense of full and truthful insight, is, it seems, a hermeneutic instrument.

In the light of these assertions, it follows truistically that understanding is a function of feeling. The structure of feeling is what it is by virtue of the reciprocal motion between itself and 'imports'. Secondly, it is so by virtue of its various constituent feelings as they play upon imports, and which it incorporates. Hence, the structure of feeling ascribes a form to what happens to us. It is bound up definitionally with its own articulation: self-and-other understanding or misunderstanding alike shape what we really feel. Thus, the interpretation of feeling is necessarily linguistic and intersubjective, and it also takes narrative shape. In short, the passions are just as much part of the momentum of public life, let alone academic scholarship, as the so-called pragmatic expediency which gets the money. Moreover, methodical human scientists, in pursuit of culture and its modes of production, would do well to avoid self-righteousness and moral hypochondria, and teach themselves a full vocabulary of the sentiments.

6

Culture and Postmodernism: The Good, the True and the Beautiful

It is finally our concern to re-view the uses and the concept of culture, with all the ambiguities and tensions of its historical constitution in the contemporary world. As I observed at the beginning of this book, word and concept are now everywhere and there can therefore be no balking this ubiquity of application, even if we have to conclude that culture has now become so vacuous a term, has to bear so many diverse deployments, covers so many references that it may be said to cover everything and therefore distinguishes nothing. A concept (with or without a word to match) serves to pick out certain identifying features and not others. It is becoming unclear what the concept culture would now exclude.

Nonetheless, we have to hand a shelf full of books on the topic and here is another one: it might be callous and would certainly be wasteful to discard it now, and make do with such neutral substitutes as 'social practice' or a medley of anthropological catch-alls like customs, rituals, routines, or habits. Culture, even when indiscriminate, retains moral force, aesthetic authority, practical usefulness; it only needs a little more care and less exercise than it usually enjoys in the business seminar or the columns of the broadsheet press.

There are always crises of understanding in history – so many, that it might be as well to think twice about using the concept of crisis quite so readily – and as many people correspondingly quick to sedate or exacerbate them with the latest jargon. Gramsci referred lugubriously to his own corner of history (one to which historians now assign some fairly confident labels) as 'an interregnum . . . full of morbid symptoms' as the new age waited to be born.[1] W. B. Yeats, in one of the most quoted poems of the twentieth century, asked in his vision of 'The Second Coming' and its parturition,

> And what rough beast, its hour come round at last,
> Slouches towards Bethlehem to be born?

The twentieth century, like most of its predecessors, was full of apocalyptic predictions, several of them credible. Now that some of the monstrous characters which strode its stage, Fascism and Stalinism among them, are dead, people look out for the new cast, and hand out the roles to whatever big names they can hire.

This, then, is the condition called postmodernity, and the postmodernists are those who offer to interpret and, by and large, to ratify it. Modernity itself is confined roughly to the epoch 1914 to 1989 (epochs are unsurprisingly tricky things to mark off: plenty which counts as modern predates 1900, plenty more still survives).

Moreover, from Theodor Adorno to Eric Hobsbawm and Jürgen Habermas, commentators on modernist culture have noted the ferocity of tension between the dark and light sides of those seventy-five years. As we saw in *The Dialectic of the Enlightenment*, Adorno pointed out the twin, contrary drives of the trust placed in reason, one which thrust towards the ruthless reduction of life to its own computation, the other which continued to grope for the conditions of emancipation and ways of keeping the promise of happiness. By the time of his death in 1969, Adorno saw the two forces converging, a lethal technicism directing all economic and political endeavour into merely technical solutions to the huge problems created by the exploitation of nature, and consumerism so saturating cultural sensibility that happiness lacked any imaginative dimension beyond the contemptible fulfilments of commodity desire and its retail therapy.

Culture itself in these veering classifications retained its bewildering, all-inclusive, glutinous and odoriferous entity. For Adorno, it included all the narratives of a society together with all that the fantasy life of their vast audiences could make of them. He, like Leavis, became convinced that commercial preference – the rank absolutism of money – had so filled to the brim the narrative resources of the whole culture that no redemption was possible other than to keep art as the sole remaining zone of obdurate resistance.

Such resistance (the echo of an electrical metaphor is relevant) could only be sustained by creating an art of extreme difficulty. In modernism, therefore, high art becomes counterposed to popular culture as the lone fount of a stern intellectuality capable of connecting with a better future, and surrounded by a commercial culture holding out a false promise of the happiness to be yielded up by the identity-rotting blandishments of kitsch, its saccharine films, television, and, above all, advertising.

II

Kitsch becomes a crux in theories of culture round about the advent of the Cold War in 1947 or so. It remains hard to define, but here it is sufficient to repeat that the narratives of kitsch culture are such as to offer the endless reassurance of a story with no painful experiences in it and only honey-covered morals to be extracted from it.

Communism and consumerism stand indicted as kitsch in each stronghold of the Cold War. The narratives of culture were enlisted by the political classes to prove to their citizens that the whole insane technology and its ideological bottom-baring was intended to protect the personal lives of the societies involved, so that their individuals could do as they liked in the playgrounds of culture, protected meanwhile by hemispheric palisades of nuclear missiles. In the age of extremes, culture is made the prime weapon of politics, on their side for the confirmation of raw power without individual value, on ours for the greater profit, naturally, as well as for the large extension and tightening of the grip of capital, not just upon the working bodies and the labour time of its employees, but upon what they supposed to be their freedoms, thoughts and ardours.

The Cold War closed in the same decade as mass production ended. The break inaugurated postmodernism. If this
dictum has the flashiness of an exam question, it is none the
worse for that. For at the end of Cold War, it seemed that the
many auguries of the century had been fulfilled, and culture
trumped politics.

In Prague in 1989 there had been for years a network of
vigorous subversives based at the Magic Lantern Theatre and
led by Vaclav Havel. Through underground drama and
fiction and forbidden film-making, as well as by those usual
means of suppressed dissent, the illicit newspaper, journal and
poster campaigns, it had kept up unbroken intellectual fire
against the dull and obdurate retention of power and maintenance of the dead old order of communism by their creature rulers. When the end came, and Mikhail Gorbachev in
Moscow declined to help out the faltering Czechoslovak government, Wenceslaus Square was filled with a jubilant crowd
of disobedient citizens whose actual but unelected leader was
Havel, an extremely principled, several-times-imprisoned
playwright-intellectual whose experience of power was
limited only to that of The Word. When free elections came,
he assumed the dark suit of the presidency with quiet grace
and modesty, and, setting himself to learn how to become a
decent shopkeeper, never lost those very qualities which by
deprecating political power conferred on him unchallenge-
able moral authority. Havel's unpresuming assumption of
office taught the extraordinary new lesson of the late twentieth century, that when culture brims over into politics
(rather than the other way round) then a generation in
whose mouths the political battle-cries of old revolution and
Enlightenment have turned filthy-tasting from dishonest use
can put its trust in culture exactly because the new dissenters
have never betrayed the word, and have refused all compromise or even contact with power. There is then the paradox
that only those imprisoned by politicians can be trusted to
practise politics, because culture has kept them clean.

A similar story can be told of the collapse of Soviet power
across central Europe in 1989,[2] one of the very greatest dates
in the calendar commemorating liberty. In each of the countries affected we find a powerful instance of how the vener-
ability of the mighty concept of culture proved such as to be
able to overthrow a seedy bunch of princes. The crux was of

course Gorbachev's rescinding of the power of the State as embodied in the tank. Once that was done, the cheerful jack-anapes of culture – teachers, journalists, playwrights, film-makers, novelists, makers of value not holders of power – dispatched the dull officers and their dour policemen. Culture's record as sign not just of a way of life but of the good, the true, and the beautiful lent it the moral authority to occupy politics.

Havel himself was therefore well placed to announce to the world, by way of the Harvard graduation address of 1995, the advent of a new civilization. 'This civilization is immensely fresh, young, new and fragile. In essence, this new, single epidermis of world civilization merely covers or con-ceals the immense variety of cultures, of peoples, of religious worlds, of historical traditions and historically formed atti-tudes, all of which . . . lie beneath it.' He noted the discor-dance between globalization and local opposition insisting on its ancient gods and the imperium of their commands, and he concluded that the world civilization would become barbarous if it could not 'do justice to the individuality of different spheres of culture' and failed to understand itself as 'multicultural and multipolar'.

'Spheres of culture' is an exacting new slogan. How are spheres to be separated? By what regulations and conven-tions do we pass between them? Politeness, as its etymology announces, is the first value of the polity. Politics must be conducted politely or it becomes as murderous as people mostly believe it to be.[3] Manners, however, are a 'sphere' of culture. Multicultural politics is therefore a matter of squar-ing good manners with a just settlement.

Such soft words are easy to agree to and even easier to become irritable with. Culture has swelled to enclose identity and to prefer itself to politics. The new name on everybody's lips, which supersedes both, is multiculturalism. Politics then becomes a rule book for the control of the upstart 'culture'.

That these are as pressing a set of concerns as any in the world, and that culture is now inignorably a matter of life and death, may be checked out at any checkpoint: between India and Pakistan, say; between Israel and the Gaza Strip; between Rwanda and Burundi; between the two halves of Belfast or Johannesburg; within Algerian, Indonesian or American families.

Multiculturalism is then the predicament postmodernism comes to solve. There are doubtless, as Perry Anderson so dazzlingly shows,[4] ample sightings of the term before 1989. In his strictly bookish history of origins, the first scripture of postmodern*ism* (where the suffix connotes not a circumstance but a social movement) is by Jean-François Lyotard in his wayward classic, *La Condition postmoderne*.[5]

Lyotard was a former Marxist militant, now persuaded of the historical irrelevance of the proletariat in a new political economy dominated not by the systems and relations of mass production, and their huge, unpredictable labour force, but by the modes and accumulations of information, knowledge and narrative.[6] In such a society the historical agency of class is superannuated; its key energies – knowledge and narrative – have no political location: they are configured in the murky, involuntary depths of culture.

Lyotard appears as first prophet of the egalitarianism of knowledges. Science, king of method and queen of objective value, has lost predominance. The relativizing of its status, by way of Heisenberg's Uncertainty Principle, Gödel's Incompleteness Theorem, and Kuhn's devastating demonstrations of its collegiate competitiveness and agonistic shifts of paradigm, deprived science of its claims to lead humankind forward by the lights of factuality, objective truth, and grounded rationality.

This was the first *grand récit* (Lyotard's phrase) of Enlightenment to fall, and with it fell rationalism's certitude of Progress, grandest of all theories of a science of society which, if dutifully followed, would lead humankind inevitably onto the uplands of reason, emancipation, and fulfilment. If such noble narratives, recited by both bourgeoisie and proletariat to their children as having the weapon of the future in their hands, no longer gripped the audience, then modernity, which launched them, was over.

In this new world, science is no longer the beacon of freedom but merely the tool of the technicists. Let us say[7] that technicism is the ideology whereby political goals are subordinated to technical efficiency, cultural values divested of creative application and dissolved into consumer choices, and aesthetic practices removed from the domain of the moral imagination and placed in the care of technique managers.

This is the disenchantment of the world announced by Max Weber at the outset of the old modernity. But the titanic struggles of beliefs and nations between 1914 and 1989 obscured just how tall and strong Weber's 'iron cage of rationality', with its rigid means-end framework, would prove to be. When the wars and rumours of wars subsided, this was the culture at the service of politics, and not the other way round. The technicists offered to manage into perfect smoothness the unpredictabilities of cultural desires, resentments and little explosions of optimism and recalcitrance. The distributions of power, privilege and wealth – Weber's trinity of politics – would, in the new reign of universal culture, be absorbed and diffused through the soft emulsions of management so that the former pains of subjugation were quite dispelled by the sweetness of opportunity, choice, and private lives.

Nothing happened quite like that. But this is Adorno's dark vision of consumer totalitarianism come to realization. The postmodernists of cultural criticism then pile in on one hand to say how awful it all is. On the other, they take the side of the happily self-indulgent crowds in the shopping mall and in front of their television sets, who are having a better time without their citizenship than they ever had before, back in the days when they were trade unionists, soldiers, mandated representatives, revolutionaries, and lively voices in the public sphere. Meanwhile, the multiculturalists of politics have nothing to say about the intrinsic worthwhileness of things. They set themselves only to think the best of other people, and teach them how to get on with one another across each and every cultural divide.

III

The most recent and compellingly simple theorist to address and condemn consumer totalitarianism in this new kind of society is David Harvey. Harvey, pursuing an insight of Robin Murray,[8] finds the cause of the postmodern rupture in the economy. The general use of the prefix 'post-' indicates how hard it is for everybody to find a way of designating the new period with new concepts. What Harvey baptizes as 'post-Fordism' describes a system of production without a mass labour force in massive factories, in which computer technology makes for productive patterns of much greater flexibility than heretofore, and in which the same instruments of communication allow workers to be at once dispersed and controlled as far afield as the globe permits. Hence sweated labour in Malaysia, Taiwan, Mozambique, Peru, Guatemala, incapable because fragmented of organized negotiation and resistance, dances to the rhythms of supply and demand in Orlando, Siena and Cheltenham. The adjective 'flexible' swiftly became the hateful cant of the epoch, and flexible structures of new production assumed instantaneously inflexible form: temporary contracts, piecework rates, casualized labour, niche marketing, accelerated obsolescence, all impelled by the immateriality of postmodern money. As never before, fabulous cascades of electronic currency pouring in and out of London, New York, Berlin, Tokyo, Singapore and Hong Kong, make history into world history. Under the banner of 'globalization' and the liturgy of free trade, deregulation, and with it the unfettered rights of private property to come and go as it likes, leaving behind the delirium of sudden wealth or the dereliction of dead industry, the torrential river of this latest phase of capitalism itself creates, in Harvey's vision, a superstructural culture to match.

In his simple mirror-image, the creatures of the system become, if they are one of its senior managers, members of a rich, rootless élite owing responsibility to no country, possessed of and by an identity scored deeply by the voluntary coercions of overwork and the momentary clichés of perfect hedonism (sun, sand, skis, sex). If, however, they are merely clerical hands subordinated to this system, they will have acquiesced to its rhythms, working longer hours than ever seemed possible when the society of infinite leisure empowered by new technology first fired sociological imaginations forty-odd years before, submitting themselves to the external and spasmodic rhythms of hiring and firing as the market veers in its moods. The post-Fordist worker obediently discards one set of work roles and the social being which goes with them, and retrains in another in front of the ghostly relations enjoined by internet and call-centre.[9]

The self created as an individual in the new proletariat of such industrialization is also someone uprooted from a local network of personal interaction; identity is no longer formed by the brotherhood of labour, neighbour, class, locality. Such a new self moves, in the Czech novelist, Milan Kundera's, phrase, with an unbearable lightness of being, obedient feather to the winds blowing from transnational competition.

If this is the new culture of selfhood, there are of course consequences for creative expression and artistic making.[10] Marxists like Harvey and Anderson, zealous to prove the decadence of late capitalism, equip us with the arguments to analyse all the things ill done and done to others' harm by the new technology and the political economy which goes with it. There is no lack of occasion for putting such a case. At the same time, human hope is pretty well inextinguishable, and plenty of people have, with equal justice, greeted the advent of postmodernism and its parent globalization with a show of enthusiasm for its liberating energies and eagerness at its informative and creativity-enhancing prowess.

Globalization is of course a crux for culture at the present time. But 'crux' means a crossing-point, mostly of the intractable kind that one has to stop at and clear away. As is usually the case, however, when large concepts present themselves to culture, they cannot be braced against it, but rather begin instead to dissolve into their vaguely constituent fragments.

So it is with globalization. The term has for a couple of decades been caught up by those eagerly and greedily anticipating a new economic world order in which all markets will be rigged under the banner of financial freedom, and the 'invisible hand' forever working to perfect the truly free competition of goods and exchange will be given unimpeded and global play. Struck, on the other hand, by the extent to which no such consequences may be seen, but rather that the invisible hand portions out the profits with an ever more brutal indifference to want and misery, a stirring of street dissent since the new millennium began has dispatched its protestants to those world capitals where senior capitalists decide what to do next with their money, in order to object vehemently to the idea of benign globalization, and to substitute for it due recognition of its deadly selfishness and globe-destroying properties.

What the concept of culture does to both contentions is blur and dissolve globalization itself into a wide variety of different mutations, as each manifestation of multinational economics reaches into and is absorbed by the customs, cognitions, committees, and significances which together make up the locations of culture.

Intellectually, no doubt, the moral of all this is simple: the tale of globalization – which, make no mistake about it, is as real as the roaring lion, going about seeking whom it may devour – must be told strictly in terms of its local arrivals and its subsequent domination ('hegemony' in the jargon) or defeat at the hands of the local market, unalike in Seoul, Marrakesh, Anchorage or Irkutsk.

The intellectual lesson is well taken; the proper use of the concept of culture rejects grand theory. But there is no reassurance for anybody in this insistence upon the contextualization of the tidal waves of global money. Whatever money does, it does powerfully, and however much the idea that local culture softens and absorbs the sheer explosiveness of new capital helps quieten one's anxiety, the fact remains that 'all history is now world history' – and never more so than when history arrives dressed up as the global future and brandishing promises of credit.

It ought to be added at this point that several non-denominational critics are in any case far from persuaded of the ultimate expansiveness of globalization,[11] whether in the economic or cultural sphere. No doubt at a time of (in Gramsci's phrase) an 'interregnum between epochs, full of morbid symptoms', we all snatch up the latest concept offering to summarize what is going on. The three critics cited are united in saying sceptically that there is less of it about than one might think: that national governments put most of their money into national investment; that 'inward investment' (that is, investment by foreign firms exporting capital to one's own country) is much smaller than globalization implies; that multinational corporations are very cautious about moving into new geographies; and that, as we have observed, even when countries are invaded by the products of other national cultures, they transmute and alter them according to local practice and preference.

For one (rather large) thing, so-called national cultures are themselves riven and bloodstained by struggles over what they really are. This has been a resonant theme of this book: cultures may indeed be, in Geertz's (and our best) thumbnail definition, 'the ensemble of stories we tell ourselves about ourselves', but those stories are only told insofar as they are victorious in the struggle for survival of everybody's favourite household words. Some stories about culture, especially with regard to its precious component, identity, are deliberately, at times cruelly suppressed, and others just peter out as the soil they thrive in (that is, the social group that tells them) radically changes its composition.

Identity crises are always with us, and may be counted as so regular a feature of the 'way of struggle' (as distinct from way of life) which *is* culture that such perturbations offer the best chance we have of studying culture in action. Arguments over identity take place on the very twistpoint of modernity, that zone of experience where what is given by one's social history, one's place in social structure (family, class), even one's very geography (the place you belong), all clash more or less noisily with what may be made of this stuff by one's self-possession.[12]

Identity is, then, an ardent but uncertain quantity, in part a chosen allegiance, in part a given membership, and it is useful – indeed, unavoidable – to find in its forms and contradictions the mass and energy of culture. Insofar, however, as we try to measure this mass as it is swept along by contemporary globalization, then identity is one form in which culture may be caught on the move.

I say 'caught', but it is part of the litany of globalization theory that its waves are too vast and momentous to be withstood by anything so cloudy as culture. We have to some extent rebutted this rapturous view: culture being the water we swim in, big waves are to be expected from time to time. Indeed, it is worth pointing out just how long-playing is the lament that tidal waves of change leave us all drowning in the dark. As far back as 1848, the French poet-politician Alphonse de Lamartine wrote in anguish, 'These times are times of chaos; opinions are a scramble; parties are a jumble;

the language of new ideas has not been created' and, a little later, from a short distance away, the historian J. A. Froude spoke of 'the intellectual lightships breaking from their moorings', envying a new generation 'which has learned to swim for itself'.[13]

Ever since there has been such a thing as a history of ideas (since Thomas Hobbes, say) there has been a vision of chaos. No doubt it is all worse just now, and certainly we have a longer list of strange and ugly new names with which to describe the loss of bearings which Marx's great ideological prose-poem, *The Communist Manifesto*, describes so eloquently: 'Everything solid melts into air, all that is holy is profaned . . .'.

Our analysts[14] speak polysyllabically and in turn of five new processes: 'deterritorialization' (culture as torn out of its geography and made homeless); 'hybridity' (cultures as mixed up together); 'liminality' (poor cultures shoved off the edge by rich ones); 'diasporization' (cultures scattered worldwide but persisting in a mutant form); above all, analysts speak of 'mediatization' (the stories of culture detached from their local habitations and carried largely abroad by the electronic media).

All these heathen tendencies may be found in action at every point of our conceptual history: Herder gave them something of a welcome, Ruskin detested them, Gramsci hoped they would provide the weapons of revolution, and more recently feminists have made a new politics out of these upheavals in culture, and thereby coined their own oxymoron, 'cultural politics'.

What is not in doubt, however, is that globalization has hugely accelerated in all these ways in the past thirty years. Discussing culture, however, strictly in terms of its being torn out of its territory, miscegenated and scattered abroad, is to stick a bit too tightly to the anthropological usage of cultures as uniform systems enclosed, and at their best, repetitious. It is also to ignore that everyday usage which refers, loosely but intelligibly, to the 'culture' of corporations, institutions and the like.

Culture may, in other words, be sliced several ways. Anthropologists may no longer be able to describe without overlap or remainder the culture of Trobriand Islanders,

Samoans or Inuit each as though untouched by the forces of globalization, but the culture of the social class charged with globalization is another matter. Natives of the new international elite, with its stupefying wealth and deadly hours of overwork, have more in common with one another across national boundaries and even languages than with compatriots who lack the money, the time, and the chance to be recruited to one of the towering gold-and-glass cathedrals of capital.

These men and women are as decidedly members of a culture as fulfilled and final as those happy naturists whose ways of life were first chronicled for richer countries by old anthropology.[15] They share the same rituals of culinary and oenological consumption, worship at the same shrines of leisure, adorn their bodies with identical suntans and cosmetics, attend the same secret ceremonies of decision-making, confirm their kinship and its exclusivity by marriage, inheritance and legislation – all this as great courtesans and captains, kings and magi, have always done. Indeed, one might suggest it as a duty to a few properly egalitarian students of culture and future stars of our subject that they set about the study of the rich and powerful by way of attempting to restrain their predatory and mostly pretty selfish purposes. In an excellently relevant critique of globalization, conducted from well within the enclaves of power, Joseph Stiglitz sketches out one preliminary such enquiry.

His purpose is to identify the most wretched of the consequences of globalization for human misery in all those many regions of the world once thought of as 'developing' of their own accord into productive nations, and now stalled, half-starved, misgoverned, and borne down ever deeper into poverty by their burden of debt.[16] The indifferent author of this catastrophe is, Stiglitz contends, the International Monetary Fund. His relevance for our purposes is that his explanation is cultural. The officers of the Fund (he is in a position to know: he was for three years chief economist at the World Bank) share, exactly and comfortably, a culture: social practices, intellectual presuppositions, business ceremonies, kinship arrangements. Moreover, they only meet, Stiglitz points out, with those people in the countries which apply for loans who pursue precisely similar ways of life.

They can insist, as they did in Jakarta in 1998, on eliminating food subsidy for the poor because they never talked to anyone without enough to eat. By the time the poor rioted, the IMF had long since left by first-class jumbo jet.

There is an intellectual difficulty here. When political critics like Stiglitz attack class privilege and the timeless presumption of the rich that their riches are the well-merited desserts of their virtues, they usually curse their opponents' errors for being merely 'ideological'. Telling ideology from culture is a tricky business, particularly since ideology has such pejorative overtones; to be ideological is notoriously to be in danger of bigotry; at its worst, ideology is merely the stooge of power. Stiglitz catches this in one strong sentence: 'While misguidedly working to preserve what it saw as the sanctity of the credit contract the IMF was willing to tear apart the even more important social contract.'[17]

What is under stricture here is the values to which IMF officials were committed, and it is my proposal, as we shall see, that the study of culture simply is the study of values in action. In which case, how shall we tell ideology apart from culture?

The answer for the anthropologist – and, it should be recalled, method is inseparable from morals – may be found in chapter 2, 'Culture and Politics'. Ideologies are nothing if not political. Ideologies offer maps of a problematic social reality and make shift with matrices for the creation of a collective consciousness.[18] They are figures on the ground of culture, and that ground provides the symbols, the metaphors, the imaginative models, the very frames of sentiment with which to enclose experience and give it meaning, out of all of which ideology may be fashioned. Culture provides those absolute presuppositions we must make about the world in order to think and feel at all. It is those attributes and materials which make us feel at home (or estranged) in our culture.

The study of ideology is then subordinate to, but inextricably part of, the study of culture, the two together being the content of the cultural politics which is both practice and discipline of the modern intellectual. Each has its peculiar form and content, but each, in the contemporary world, can only be made visible through the lenses of the other. Thus, I under-

stand, for example, the weird self-ignorance, stupendous generosity and wilful blindness of American politics by way of
the cultural history of Federalists and oil millionaires, Hollywood movies and Louisiana farmers. The reverse way imaginatively to grasp the power of the French state, to take an
illuminating example, as it functions so hugely, benignly,
chauvinistically in medical policy is to listen to the story of
its DNA research[19] and the peculiarly French idealism with
which money was raised and profits refused in the race to
map the human genome. The French were stoutly of the view
that human biological materials should not be objects of commerce; as in Britain, blood used in genome research was a
gift. The international drug companies were bemused. The
French cabinet risked French lives by protecting French
science. Accusations of exploitation were broadcast from all
sides. Mutual and recriminatory misunderstanding polluted
the pure air of experimental science.

IV

This is the opportunity of the multiculturalist, in particular
when she is dressed in the robes of postcolonialist. Postcolonial theories of culture are much disfigured, as Edward Said
points out, by a politics of blame.[20] Not that there is not
plenty to blame colonialists or international bankers for –
for cruelty, greed, vindictiveness, indifference – but that the
weight of blame often contracts and distorts the interpretative circle cast around the history of empire. If we take Seyla
Benhabib as ideal type of our postcolonial theorist,[21] we find
her both strikingly tolerant and strikingly ready to issue
ethical and juridical maxims in relation to her theory (and of
a kind consistently called for by the convictions expressed
here).

That is to say, Benhabib redefines the realm of democracy
as at once political and cultural, and argues that 'the "background culture" which surrounds and infuses the task of
reason with particular content, must be considered essential
to consensus formation in liberal democracies'. She goes on:
'Deliberative democracy focuses on social movements, and on

the civil, cultural, religious, artistic and political movements of the *unofficial* public sphere as well.'[22]

Her postcolonialism (to call it that) is addressed to political principles; she dissolves the democratic difficulty by pouring politics into culture. In Benhabib's global multiculturalism we will get on with one another by greeting and saluting each other's culture, as we would when invited to each other's houses. If culture is a homely house, it is also a home which may be sold, or left, or abandoned, and is in any case very unlikely any longer to be the place where one's grandchildren will grow up.

The lesson of all this extends that of chapter 2: culture is to be found everywhere one may point it out; politics provides the rules of its ordering, and should always be a few paces behind it. Our theorist of culture, therefore, leaves the regulation of politics to the political moralist and, endowed by now with a much larger brief as to the realm and significance of culture, sets off to see what contents he or she may find with which to advance the new codes of respect for the difference of others (taught by anthropology), dialogues of compromise amidst mutual incomprehension (taught by liberal pedagogy), surprising narratives of identity-formation which abruptly alter all one's moral bearings (taught by literature), novel productions and versions of cultural expression (taught by sociology). In the postmodern era (whatever name we discover for it): 'the borderline work of culture demands an encounter with "newness" that is not part of a continuum of past and present. It creates a sense of the new as an insurgent act of cultural translation.'[23]

Spokespeople for postmodernism were able to criticize their predecessors for bowing before the pessimistic prophecies of doom in modernism, for their intolerance towards the cheerful pluralism of modern narrative, for their patriarchal authoritarianism about new narrative forms (film and television) and their narrow exaltation of word over image. The postmodernists, as one of their more voluble prophets, Fredric Jameson, contends, side without hesitation with political progressivists, eliding (as they ought) culture with politics precisely because late capitalism has done this for them. If they do not respond in the same terms the economy will appropriate the domain of personal freedom all to itself.

Jameson lists as the liberating aspects of postmodernism: 'its populism and pluralising democratisation, its commitment to the ethnic and the plebeian, and to feminism, its anti-authoritarianism and anti-élitism, precisely its anti-bourgeois features.'[24] Jameson remains some kind of Marxist, hence gets a *frisson* from shouting abuse at the bourgeoisie wherever he can. (One would have thought, on the contrary, that his list minutely characterizes every one of the clichés spoken by bourgeois readers of the English *Guardian* or the American *Vanity Fair*.)

Postmodernism, apt as all new doctrines are to self-righteousness, finds in Jameson's list, as in Benhabib's precepts, not only ethical principles about how to live, but formal ones about how to create. Its preferred forms stigmatize all kinds of finality, particularly of narrative and its actions, as unattainable 'closure'. The same forms dissolve the 'essentialist' nature of character and value, finding all social and personal qualities to be 'constructed' (in other words, in part at least, voluntary), and all aspects of personal identity to be mobile, provisional, self-sponsored. Postmodernism in this guise condemns the fixed self and its strong embodiment in a subjectivity for its unresponsiveness to happy accident, indicts it for its supposition of its own hierarchical integrity, and blackguards it in any event for its male assertiveness and its magicking of the weapon of the phallus into the wardenship of the Word.

It cannot be doubted that postmodernism has not only issued (whether as self-conscious expressions of the movement or not) in some magnificent works of literature;[25] it has also inspired highly original works of literary commentary and moral-philosophic reflection. The conception of reader-response theory, in which the critic, sometimes helped out by empirical questioning, establishes just how inevitably creative the reader herself has to be when accommodating the author's fiction, is one rich area of productive speculation which also affirms the freedoms and inventiveness of all collaborators in culture. By the same token, the attack upon the courtroom severities of canonical judgement has done much of a generous-hearted kind to expand the pleasure of those texts once considered beneath respectable notice (children's fiction, adults' soap opera), as well as to welcome with a similar

hospitality culture expressed by peoples excluded from cano-
nicality by such disqualifications as wrong colour, wrong
gender, wrong class; low language, alien country, forbidden
topics.

Profanity is dangerous, sanctity pure. Postmodernism
deliberately profanes culture. Or rather, postmodernism
declares that it has discovered what culture has now become.

Richard Rorty may be said to have initiated the argument
of the period as well as to have fixed the fulcrum[26] on which
the balance of an era tipped. He reinterpreted the most
formidable of the old physicalist (that is, hard-scientific)
philosophers to show that the fundamental conditions
required for a theory of knowledge which would exactly
reflect, as if in a mirror, the realities of the natural world,
were impossible of attainment. Rorty was the formidable
demolition-man who broke up the foundation of a founda-
tional philosophy of knowledge. Insofar as the human sciences shared the ambition to ground themselves as objectively
as, it was believed, the hard sciences had done, then their
foundationalism was even more completely exploded than in
the laboratories. Rorty asks in some exasperation, of those
people who separate the world of thinkers into idealists and
materialists, 'What is this mental physical contrast anyway?
Whoever said that anything one mentioned had to fall into
one or other of two (or half-a-dozen) ontological realms?'[27]

It is a point well taken. Postmodernism and good sense
alike do for the distinction. It actively obstructed a sufficiently
faithful insight into the 'universal dovetailedness' (the phrase
belongs to Dickens) of human practices. Once Wittgenstein
had shown how supple and variegated were the purposes to
which human beings bent their language in efforts to conjure
the world, and brought out so emphatically how public, disputable, embodied, and active its meanings are, materialism
and idealism together collapsed into culture. What is then
required is a much thicker, subtler, more resourceful vocabulary of description for the contents of that culture.

Such a vocabulary and a rhetorical ear to match would be
able to call up the weightiness and wit, the heaviness of being
and the vitality of seeing to be found on almost any page of
the writers reviewed with critical approbation in these pages.
Their common language of cultural theory and practice, of a

close and vivid description which carries with it its own 'strong evaluations', in their very work constituting and renewing culture, itself charges up the people nourished by that culture. The common language of Evans-Pritchard and Leavis, Hoggart and Geertz, John Ruskin and Raymond Williams, Benjamin and Benedict has, no doubt, its disciplinary requirements and its scholastic obscurity. But in a way simply not the case with, say, political science, management technique, or the cleverness which passes understanding amongst the Parisian pentecostals, the language of cultural enquiry and method is capable of speaking of matters of life and death seriously, lightheartedly, in detail and with a tough connection between passion and action.

Listing those august names, however, implies no call to follow an antique drum backwards into reaction. Williams does not repeat Ruskin's homilies; the ardour of the identity debate stands at a long remove from Margaret Mead's typification of Balinese character or Richard Hoggart's loving portrait of working-class matriarchs; the black writer of the postmodernist day – as varied a representative trio as V. S. Naipaul, Derek Walcott and Toni Morrison – kneels to the names of W. E. B. Dubois and Ida B. Wells, but the structure of feeling (in the phrase) peculiar to postmodernism is keenly present to us now. The theoretical consequences announced by its priesthood may be disputable, but its declaration of the advent of relativism is unignorable. So I shall say that the form and content of relativism and what it has done to change our minds (and therefore our culture) offer the readiest opportunity to understand the nameless epoch of postmodernity and the delusions of globalization.

V

There are truths in relativism;[28] it has happened to our sensibilities, and done so at least partly as a result of the spread of anthropological knowledge and democratic experience brought by global economics. It is not, however, a free-standing ethical doctrine; it is a cadence (or an aura) of moral thought, and must be listened to. Efforts to turn relativism into a set of premisses lead straight to self-contradiction and, despite the best efforts of the more mad-eyed and deconstructive postmodernists, reason and its rules remains the only aid we have with which to keep horror at bay and the world in order. If, on the other hand, there can truly be no such monster in scientific enquiry (or everyday life) as the objective, disengaged, clinically observing self, it follows that all of the study of culture depends on the moments of collision between us and other people. Otherness (sometimes 'alterity') is the concept coined to accommodate such collisions.

It is this mutual shock of meeting difference and the subsequent repulse from it for which relativism offers its new moral-political context. To summarize: the relativist holds that all human action must be evaluatively understood only in relation to its precise context. (As this stands, it would be a premiss of any serious morality.) Secondly, the relativist holds (or very strongly and habitually implies) that the cultures which supply this context are self-identifying and enclosed systems. From this it follows that the moral element in the collision between oneself and the other must be simply suspended. Whatever others do, they do for their own good reasons, and there is nothing we can or should do about it other than accept it. Indeed, such acceptance is then enjoined upon us as a moral (although non-relative) obligation.

There are standard objections to all these positions. In the first, as remarked, interpretative contextualization is a feature of any human enquiry as well as of any humane ethics. In the second, also as much remarked in chapter 3, modernity has made all cultures and most national frontiers porous; modern communication systems, above all television and jumbo jets, have made those nations wealthy enough to watch or fly them familiar with all kinds of once-exotic otherness, and made those at the other end of the camera or the flight path no longer puzzled or embarrassed at being gazed at with an anthropologist's or a tourist's or a United Nations soldier's eye. Thirdly, it should be pointed out to the relativist that there is a logical inconsistency, in that any relativizing precept requires the non-relative justification that relativism be universalized.

The relativist in reply may sensibly do away with this objection by saying that only the principle of toleration of alien practices is to be absolute, as being the best non-coercive guarantee of the relativity of life within the circle of its protection. This is a sort of one-precept-and-then-relativism with which to protect cultures too much interfered with in the past.

One might think of such a procedure as honest pruden-tialism allied to a nice politics of politeness, and, indeed, some such alliance comes near to being the best sort of beginning to a peaceful-minded global ethics. But it lacks content. Rel-ativism (and its postmodern proponents) is quite right to say that the individualizing of values, which is the inevitable product of any globalization which does *not* transform poli-tics into a system for management by moral technology is no more than a common acknowledgement of the dozens of maps of local knowledge still guiding conduct. The trouble is that these are now detached from past and future. The old traditions of morality and civic education which provided these maps with their bearings, pathways, and landmarks, can no longer do so, or only do so for abruptly foreshortened journeys. Efforts to force them on people lead to terror and torture.

Now the fact[29] of moral and value differences between societies or cultures cannot be made to yield a principle of non-interference. It is a feature of moral theory as of any other kind of theory that it seeks to universalize its account of human action. Since it is also a fact of the modern world that it is irreversibly interdependent, it is not surprising that almost the only universal currency of moral exchange is a doctrine of rights, since these are moral properties to which peoples of very different moral traditions can make ready appeal without committing themselves any further about the content of those freedoms and sanctities conferred by rights. Relativism, after all, is here to stay; postmodernity and glob-alization, whatever one says they are, have dissolved so many fixed positions and dug up such a lot of deep-rooted bound-aries, that keeping social method, political expedience and moral principle conjoined is going to be a difficult business. It will be best conducted according to those deliberately short-sighted principles of the culturalists: sort out the particulars, interpret the local narratives, struggle for a compromise between the facts and values of savage conflict, and sketch an account of how each side may rationally co-exist.

Let us say it again. *The study of culture is not the same thing as the practice of politics.* These admonitions of the previous paragraphs are no more than a few tips on how to ward off charges of high-minded ineffectuality, and to suggest the relevance of cultural method to the contriving of our elusive science of human affairs. Culture as our topic and cultural enquiry as our method have the strengths of relevance and fascination; culture is the water we all swim in, and the news of the world an ensemble of narratives describing all the different lakes, rivers, and oceans in which everybody else takes their dip. Politicians teach us to swim; analysts of culture, if they do it for a living, are, I suppose, their teaching assistants.

Water being so hospitable an environment, many different creatures live in it. The overwhelming demands of a globalized world require us to see and evaluate far more of our environment – geographical, economic, moral – than ever before. This is what it is to live in the information age, and this is why the practice of politics must now so depend upon the study of culture, for all that in the name of reason it must also keep up a stout and workable distinction between the two.

The cultural saturation of politics, however, has as much led to the recovery of old, neglected elements in the waters of life as it has to inanity and bloatedness for those taking culture along with huge doses of self-pity or self-righteousness. It has been the mighty contribution of theoretical feminism which followed the movement's practical and political effectiveness, to identify and restore to consciousness forces in the cultural waters which fairly drove society along without anybody's noticing what they were.

It is important at this stage in such a book as this not to fall into that leaden propensity of academic discourse to substitute a directory of names for an argument. Out of the gallant regiment of women, therefore, who have effected these changes of attitude, of material examined, of judgements widely assented to, a short roster will have to serve to indicate how postmodernism and its welter of self-interpretations as often leads to effective actions for improvement as it does to the mind-poisoning mischief of academic substance-abuse. The weight of the world is such that theories of the inevitability of personal helplessness have a strong appeal and a wide audience. When such a theory is couched in the cleverness which passes understanding, then one may match one's natural indolence to happy superiority without having to display the moral relevance of one's studies.[30]

It has largely been feminist philosophers who have brought about the practical redefinitions of culture which make their case. This implicates topics as large and circumambient as culture itself: the place of women and the meaning of the feminine in the globalized world. Femininity is as pervasive and disputable as our key concept, and enters so abruptly into our meditations because it did so just as abruptly as did the general intellectual recognition that modernism was over, along with the big, cocksure political doctrines which used it to justify pretty well anything. The political movement of feminism goes back, at least, to Jane Austen and Mary Wollstonecraft; the Suffragettes were at their peak a century ago; but the specifically cultural inflections won so very hard by feminists are perhaps only thirty or so years old, and are so important here principally by virtue of their being consciously planned and doggedly worked for by a feminist intelligentsia.

A proper history at this juncture of the uncompleted revolution of feminism would require a quite different, much longer book than this. What may usefully be said is that the great change in the structures of popular feeling and their cultural expressions inaugurated (as a convenient and emblematic date) by the popular theatre of 1968 coincided with (and was in part caused by) the sharp rise in the numbers of women going to higher education in all the wealthy countries, and by far larger proportions than ever before of those same women going on to become academics, writers, broadcasters, leading figures in the cultural industries.

This quite new social formation had to cast around for heroines in a supporting history, and found Virginia Woolf and Vera Brittain in literary London and Labour politics, then Dorothy Hodgkin a little later in hard science and the peace movements, Celia Johnson on the screen and Grace Wyndham Goldie behind it at the BBC. A celebration of these figures (and a repudiation of their male rivals, wardens, and oppressors) constituted that part of the redefinition of culture on behalf of women best epitomized by the founding of the publishing house, Virago. Virago belied its sardonic self-appellation by the generosity and lavishness of its publishing programme, restoring to print a truly extraordinary range of often-forgotten, nonetheless classic works by women. It was, as the phrase goes, an intervention in culture of strategic and military proportions, and no-one can doubt it changed the culture at large.

Virago effected this victory by the sheer weight of its books. As such it is something of a baby elephant in the small argument of this book, which mostly traces the always contradictory making of a concept by way of individual usages in particular academic writing. The new books, Virago's among them, but also a huge wave from across the Atlantic and the Pacific – Kate Millett, Andrea Dworkin, bell hooks, Germaine Greer[31] – gave the movement intellectual mass, but it found its first energy, as well it might, in the universal fact of motherhood and the mother's indispensability to absolutely everyone, none more so than the little boy who would grow up to return mother to the kitchen and the bedroom and insist on running the public show by himself. The feminists who renewed the intellectual argument during and after the late 1960s turned first for cultural weaponry to the psychoanalysts of infancy, and found in Anna Freud, Susan Isaacs and Melanie Klein the materials with which they vastly extended the definition of culture in both everyday and intellectual life. Luce Irigaray, Nancy Chodorow and Jessica Benjamin[32] from the next generation are deservedly credited with resituating culture in the body and the bedroom; in childhood and in fantasy; above all, in the passions and our very strongest evaluations of them: in love. The literary critics, almost alone in the human sciences, had devised a vocabulary for the description of feelings and had insisted upon feelingful responses as the ground of their labours. But their account of what Descartes's great essay called 'the passions of the soul' – wonder, love, hatred, desire, joy, sadness[33] – was subordinate to the awfulness of judgement, and the sentences that judgement as to value passed down.

The feminists acknowledged the absolute necessity of coming to a judgement, but they did so with a kindlier disposition and a keen sense of how the passions change one's mind and therefore the culture. Pretty well by themselves, the feminists put the passions close to the centre of the study of culture, and noted as they did so the radical reordering of values such a change must cause. We should salute a handful of the philosophers who exemplify such efforts, lending themselves as they do to the methodological contention of my argument that the study of culture just *is* the study of values-in-action.[34] The student of culture will be herself pleased, I hope, that the topic of the passions and the cognate methods it enjoins blur so many academic genres and ensure such happy indisciplinarity in the way we think now.

Annette Baier and Onora O'Neill together instantiate a line of work which, in revising the hierarchy of social values, itself alters the specific gravity of culture as it presses on us all. They object that a preoccupation with justice as prime value of any society is partly a historical accident owing everything to Plato's 2,600-year-old authority, and partly a male preoccupation with the masculine realm of public retribution and distribution. Baier and O'Neill, pointing out that John Locke said the same thing, place the value of trust at the heart of the social order, and name Hume's 'civil affections' as the cultural site of its protection.[35] Their ally is Martha Nussbaum who has persevered, in an astonishing range of books,[36] in a venture to show what all but womanly men omit from their cultural and political reasoning, which is to say, the passions themselves.

It is a powerful reproach. Men run the world and, as John Stuart Mill pointed out a century and a half ago, run it publicly for themselves while running women to keep private life comfortable. Nussbaum theorizes the inevitability of a passionate presence in all social thought, and points to the distortions effected in all our understanding by the fatuous male pretence of objective rectitude and businesslike rationality. Against the dominion of scientific management, Nussbaum counterposes the knowledge accessible only to the great name of love, which she sees both as the product of a congenial culture and, insofar as it is comprehending and comprehensive enough, a guard against stupidity. The conclusions of this chapter and the last suggest one way of taking these lessons to heart. The feminists restore to the argument the idealizing ends of culture. Absorbing their arguments changes the concept once more.

Aligning the feminists' several tales is, cognitively and emotionally, more than a matter of looking at the different views, and deciding where each one stops. It is of the nature of powerful moral or scientific views, arising as they do from 'strong evaluations', that they illuminate the whole perspective. We look along the beam and cannot look outside it at what remains in the dark. But it is also of the nature of consciousness that disconcerting differences encountered in that view affect consciousness itself. Surprise is unignorable; that is the force of *difference*. The question is then to know what to do with difference, and it has always been a mark of ordinary sympathy, let alone wisdom, to recognize that one has to do *something* about it.

The whole matter is sometimes too much compounded by quoting cultural circumstances so utterly discrepant with our own that comparativism stalls. The way of life and even the art of, say, Mayan people in Central America a millennium ago are so remote that describing their culture is bound to be more formal than sympathetic – like, as one might say, describing how colour looks to a blind man.[37] Difference then becomes less a matter of drawing boundaries on the other side of which we find the Other, and more a matter of scale. Mayans are so far off and tiny we can discern very little, none of it illuminating, most of it, as we say, anecdotal.

The heaven and the hell of the study of culture is that each of us is in it and of it, made by it at the same time as making something of it. This being so, then changeable and not-so-changeable as human beings are, neutrality in the science of culture is quite unfeasible. The observer-participant observes through the value-optics of the day, for most of us, most likely, the optics of social democracy. And so holding to its venerable principles and sentiments – state neutrality in religion, sufficient social justice, hopeful egalitarianism, belief in emancipation for men and women, respect for the canons of scientific knowledge, enlightenment values all of them – the human scientist in all of us carries them aloft into his or her participation in culture, whether as its student, guest, citizen or critic.

VI

We cannot do without culture and we cannot do with it. It is an indispensable moral weapon with which to invent and mark off such precious values as identity and ethnicity; at the same time, it is obvious to those both in and outside the particular versions of such values to hand that much cant is uttered under their protection.

It was never easy to escape self-righteousness in cultural commentary, nor other such sins of egocentric commission as condescension, straight and inverted snobbery, rhetorical vulgarity, and discourtesy amounting to cruelty. Culture as a so very contested concept is the more prone to prompt such offences precisely because it touches so nearly the touchiest zones of being, those where personal taste abuts self-esteem; where identity, both willed and given, draws strength from custom and ceremony; where the sense of self muscles in on membership and tones up along the boundary keeping Them away from Us.

These are the spectacles of culture, to be looked at and through. So it is an inadequate response simply to become exasperated by the ubiquity of the word – although one certainly sees why people do – and to suggest that one substitute value-neutral terms which may prevent the argument being simply directed at that part of the audience which will clap the loudest. To return the content of our concept to the spectacle is, no doubt, to underline the contemporaneity of our concern with culture. If we set ourselves to distinguish finally (in this book at least) the domains of culture and politics, it will not be to put down either to the advantage of the other. Nor will any such distinction aim to prevent present licentiousness in typifying this or that as 'a culture of . . .'. When, for instance, Christopher Lasch spoke his wholesale malediction over the condition of America, he coined an early sighting of the usage: he called his book *The Culture of Narcissism.*[38]

In doing so he aimed to catch in one net the several fish swimming in the culture, staining its waters with gluey self-absorption, magnetizing it with sentimental egoism, fertilizing the thick seaweeds of euphemism, self-pitying evasiveness, all-enveloping emotionalism. Lasch was cavalier with his evidence, but one cannot doubt that he had a catch, and one to be made as much in Northern Europe as in the United States. Robert Hughes, no less crudely and with as clenched a fist, hit *Culture of Complaint*[39] in much the same way a dozen years later. He indicted *a* culture (not *the* culture) for its moral hypochondria, neurotic sensitivity to slights, self-pitying obsessionality with always-disputable questions of identity, ethnic or otherwise, mere indifference to tell the harder facts of poverty, sickness, misery and death. Richard Rorty then followed in his turn,[40] this time reproaching no-less-sentimental Leftists for forgetting the proper liturgy of socialism and its attention to the political brutalities of class injustice and inequality, substituting instead the cultural vaguenesses of linguistic insult, identity violation, and a social marginality enforced not by the imperialism of guns and policemen, but by the imagination.

Each writer implied an everyday definition of culture, usable, necessary, palpable, elusive. Each insisted on the heavy presence of value in the concept. In any of its meanings, domestic or aesthetic, semiotic or ethical, culture carries values. To say so is to move the term clear away from value-neutral competitors like 'social practices' and from technicalities taken from theoretical linguistics, such as 'orders of signification'. Values condense the general term 'meaning' into something at once more inflammable, more weighted down with historical gravity, loaded up with usefulness, as a weapon or as a medicine. Meanings mean, of course; values do.

Culture, therefore, is a structure of values and of the feelings which belong to them, moving through a force field of social action. Politics is the pattern of relations into which the society in question falls, as its members both resist and express its culture. Neither is predominant; either is a tissue of narratives; primacy is a consequence of human effort and accident. Sometimes culture wins out, sometimes politics, either for better or worse. As Wolf Lepenies points out,[41] culture may be used as an excuse when politics disgraces itself. German *Kultur* – 'German idealism, the classic literature of Weimar, and the classical and romantic styles in music [which] preceded the founding of the political nation by more than a hundred years'[42] – has been regularly used as a sanctum of 'inwardness', redeeming the Germans from the all-too-outward and atrocious monstrosity of their Nazi politics. Lepenies will have nothing to do with 'the elevation of culture and the degrading of politics'; a society is responsible to and for the latter in a way it cannot be for its culture.

The deep difficulty with culture, as this book has been at pains to bring out, is its all-or-nothingness. The corresponding exigency of politics is its collapsing absolutely everything in front of power. Make a fetish of power and all you can stand on is the powerlessness of principle; do the same with culture, and your only principle is one of moral superciliousness.

Politics is the practical business of societies, and power only one of its quantities. Culture is the evaluative activity of everyday life, and efficacity not really an issue. Let us say that a culture may be operationally defined as dominant-values-plus-explanatory-system.[43] Thus, the task in hand will be to identify that smallish cluster of key values (dominant, residual, emergent) by which a culture takes its bearings, and then trace how they animate and direct its system of explanation, its identification of reasons and causes, its distinguishing between means and ends.

VII

Perhaps we have now come to a working definition of culture which takes in enough of its many usages and their lessons for experience as canvassed in this book. *Let the study of culture be the study of enacted values as each assumes its place in the narrative of the day.* This allows us to heed the anthropologists when they throw such a medley of strange social activities into the stewpot of culture, and further to insist that when we take them out we notice how little the bits of life have actually melted together, and how contrastive they remain.

'The study of enacted values' – a paraphrase of Clifford Geertz's phrase already quoted – 'a constellation of enshrined ideas', keeps us alert to the movement of these values through history, and therefore to their unabsolute temporality. Values come and change and go; they emerge, command, and fade; they conflict, sometimes violently, and become covered with blood. Seeing bloodstains brings us up with a jolt. Such a jolt returns us to that segment in the concept of culture which stores up our ideals, and reminds of the conflicts they cause. We match our opponents with the best we have known and thought.

'Have thought?' But might not the best still be to come? The perfectionist argument is far from dead, even if culturalists and sociologists become rather embarrassed these days when it is mentioned. Stanley Cavell, going back to the great American idealist, Ralph Waldo Emerson, remarks that Emerson, like the German Nietzsche, would curse official culture for its very pastness, for casting the best that is in us in terms of what has been rather than what might be.[44] We know the best in terms of what has been known and thought already of course, but we also know that our self-dissatisfaction stems from a desire 'for something higher . . . a higher self as yet still concealed'.

Cavell is at pains to wrest from Nietzsche an account which may be used to vindicate anti-egalitarian beliefs in the individual's self-defining unco-operative immutuality. He takes from Nietzsche and gives to Emerson the fine phrase, 'the domestication of culture', and does so in the name of democracy. If we are to have the mutually responsible world without which neither peacefulness nor justice, trust nor happiness, will be possible, the best of culture must be able to live with the worst of democracy. 'Each philosopher,' Cavell quotes Emerson as saying, 'has only done, as by a delegate, what one day I can do for myself'.[45] The domestication of culture will have been accomplished when you and I do the philosophy for ourselves.

Cavell repudiates those who claim that this version of perfectionism is just old religious redemption in a secular surcoat. He quotes from Emerson's great essay 'Self-reliance': 'In every work of genius we recognize our own rejected thoughts. They come back to us with a certain alienated majesty.'[46] He goes on to return self-dissatisfaction and the aspiration it betokens to the world of 'education and character and friendship', in part as preparation for the ways in which democracy is certain to disappoint us (but must not be dispensed with), more largely because it is only in terms of these that a usable image of perfectionism in culture may be created and lived. For these purposes, a great book or film becomes a great friend, even while remaining a master; great friendship brings out, we hope, the best in us. Rather than art, it is our best token of what culture can do.

We have now operationalized (as they say) our concept in readiness for a finale. Jürgen Habermas[47] warns us that modern capitalism has split culture into life-world and systems-world, and has devised a politics to match each hemisphere. Life-world is leisurely and cultural, systems-world regulatory and productive, but the second overflows into the first, even as we all try to hold it back. Modernity itself has invaded the looked-for happinesses of private lives with the armies of administration and pervaded them with the viruses of commercialism. Postmodernism, attempting a rhetoric of gaiety and playfulness, has proved helpless to organize a cultural resistance.

Old Enlightenment taught that the mighty languages of science, politics, art, would be so spoken by all citizens that they would at once command their own politicians and create their own culture. Habermas concludes that, relentlessly driven on by capital and its technology, each knowledge-sphere has become indecipherably specialized, and the dependent values of each – truth, justice, beauty – removed from popular diction.

Habermas's diagram of the present will help to give us our bearings after the exhilaration of Cavell. Anybody might be despondent these days about the prospects for emancipation, self-critical self-awareness, the retrieval of art from kitsch, of politics from technicism, of science from destruction, of democracy from tyranny. A monograph on culture, however, can afford to point at the possibility of perfectionism still managing to breathe. Culture, as it has been repeatedly defined in these pages, is 'the ensemble of narratives we tell ourselves about ourselves'. The study of culture *on its own terms* is therefore the study of our values as enacted to fit the plot of our social narratives. They may be found anywhere – in casual conversation, in the routines of all institutions, in ordinary sociability and exchange, in the moral imagination of society. The student of culture, whether anthropologist, sociologist, literary critic or just plain common reader, politician or citizen, looks for the lived values and the enshrined ideas and, by interpreting them, judges and incorporates them into his or her sense of, let us say, the best things in life and the happiest days each can imagine.

Beyond question, for most of us and certainly for a student, the readiest place to find these narratives is television, and although the enacted narratives of television are no doubt imaginary, they formidably constitute the stuff of culture without exhausting culture. Guy Debord told us forty years ago that we had entered upon 'the society of the spectacle',[48] and no-one can doubt that our culture, for all its chattiness, is now more visual than verbal, and that students now coming to university are more intensely and sharply accomplished in reading images than speaking or writing words.[49]

For the purposes of a conclusion, therefore, let us concede the commonplace that *everyone* contrives their own explanatory anthropology for the accommodation of television, *and* carries it over into everyday encounters as well. Television narratives, so awful and so sentimental, so universal *and* so full of aspirations for heightened life, serve us for the moment as type and token of all the narratives of culture.

Matters can hardly be left there, of course. For all that the *average* number of hours spent in Britain in front of the television now hovers at over thirty a week[50] for those in employment or at school (far more for those not), the nature and quality of the experience of watching, as anybody knows from introspection, is very varied. Raymond Williams, in a sharp-tongued essay, took the measure of the distance between our watching, their reporting, and the lives and deaths caught on camera. These things fluctuate.[51] Some images catch and hold some people painfully or joyfully, others leave us indifferent. Some television dramas, like great novels, remain in the mind and its feelings forever, changing the very cadences of one's character: Troy Kennedy Martin's *Edge of Darkness*, Dennis Potter's *Pennies from Heaven* (these are classics of culture). The immediacy and inescapability of television is the point, however. If we seek out the stories we tell ourselves about ourselves, there they are. That

is the place for our new kind of cultural student, the anthropologist of everyday life, to make a start. All the discriminations are still to be made, no doubt: as to what people do
with what they watch according to old catch-alls like age and
class and sex and colour, but in front of the screen, the
unquenchable ardour to learn the truth, to adjudicate the
good, and to love the beautiful, bubble spontaneously up or
dribble uselessly away. No doubt the discrepancy between
much of what is shown and the ideal trinity of beauty, truth
and goodness is often raucously comic. But people go unre-
pentantly on making the discriminations, finding things beautiful, wanting them to be just, believing them to be true.

In her affecting reaffirmation of these needful activities,
Elaine Scarry writes (in Emersonian accents): 'Something
beautiful fills the mind yet invites the search for something
beyond itself, something larger or something of the same
scale, with which it needs to be brought into
relation . . . What is beautiful is in league with what is
true because truth abides in the immortal sphere . . .'. She
continues:

> the beautiful person or thing incites in us the longing for truth
> because it provides by its compelling 'clear discernibility' an
> introduction (perhaps our first introduction) to the state of
> certainty yet does not itself satiate our desire for certainty
> since beauty, sooner or later, brings us into contact with our
> own capacity for making errors . . . the beautiful, almost
> without any effort of our own, acquaints us with the mental
> event of conviction, and so pleasurable is this that ever after-
> wards one is willing to labor, struggle, wrestle with the world
> to locate . . . what is true . . . beauty is the starting place for
> education.[52]

Cultural theorists may be shy of both beauty and truth
these days, but in ordinary lives, ordinary people are not.
Those 'inherent and inextinguishable attributes of the human
mind' invoked by Wordsworth will go on searching for truth,
goodness, justice, and beauty, however embarrassed about it
some of their sometime-mentors may become.

It will be a bad day when the narratives of television fail
to yield up a sufficient range of programmes for the correct

application of our noblest ideals. It will be even grimmer if educators come to suppose that such ideals are, in the teeth of the worst that old corruption or new fundamentalism can do, moribund. Darkest of all would be the supposition that, having survived the deadliest that the twentieth century could do, teachers of the newest generation, shining like its predecessors with cheerfulness and hope, could only tell their children that all was lost, culture and beauty and truth were lost, and all they had to give them was money.

Notes

Chapter 1   Birth of a Concept

1   Peter Berger and Thomas Luckmann, *The Social Construction of Reality*, Harmondsworth: Allen Lane, Penguin Press (1967).
2   John Searle, *The Construction of Social Reality*, London: Allen Lane (1995).
3   Oscar Lewis, *The Culture of Poverty*, New York: Holt Rhinehart (1963).
4   Particularly by J. L. Austin in his *Philosophical Papers*, ed. J. O. Urmson and G. J. Warnock, Oxford: Clarendon Press (1961), ch. 1, esp. pp. 1–17.
5   Quentin Skinner, 'Language and Social Change', in his *Meaning and Context*, ed. J. Tully, Princeton: Princeton University Press (1988), p. 120.
6   Ibid. p. 120.
7   The *Oxford English Dictionary* (1979 edition) is of course resolutely descriptive in its system.
8   This is a very simplified summary of Karl Popper's two classics: *The Logic of Scientific Discovery*, London: Routledge and Kegan Paul (1953); *Conjectures and Refutations*, London: Routledge and Kegan Paul (1966).
9   The quoted phrases are those best known today from Sprat's famous manifesto, 'History of the Royal Society', here taken from Basil Willey's indispensable textbook, *The Seventeenth Century Background*, Harmondsworth: Penguin (1964), pp. 186–95.
10   Perhaps Rousseau's most famous slogan, to be found in his *Social Contract* (1762): J.-J. Rousseau, *The Social Contract*

and Discourses, ed. G. D. H. Cole, London: Dent (1938). For the tradition in which he worked, see also John Passmore, *The Perfectibility of Man*, London: Duckworth (1970).

11   The phrases quoted are from Immanuel Kant, *The Critique of Pure Reason*, trans. L. W. Beck, Indianapolis: Bobbs-Merrill (1954).

12   This was also the title of a study of its later Victorian practitioners. See John Burrow, Stefan Collini, and Donald Winch, *That Noble Science of Politics*, Cambridge: Cambridge University Press (1983).

13   We owe a great debt to Isaiah Berlin for his re-affirmation of Herder's importance in his *Vico and Herder: Two Studies in the History of Ideas*, London: Hogarth Press (1976). Phrases from Herder are quoted here from his *Ideas for a Philosophy of Human History* (1791): *J. G. Herder on Social and Political Culture*, ed. F. M. Barnard, Cambridge: Cambridge University Press (1969).

14   Quoted by Berlin, *Vico and Herder*, pp. 187–8.

15   The title of an essay by Bernard Williams, printed in his *Moral Luck*, Cambridge: Cambridge University Press (1981).

16   Berlin, *Vico and Herder*, p. 193.

17   He is praised in this role as a scholarly opponent of westernizing the East by Edward Said in his *Orientalism*, Harmondsworth: Penguin (1985), pp. 98, 118.

18   Herder wrote a study entitled 'The Voices of Peoples (*Völker*) in Their Songs' – one of the first scholarly essays on popular music: *Herder on Social and Political Culture*, pp. 79–88.

19   Henri Matisse in R. Goldwater and M. Treves (eds), *Artists on Art*, New York: Pantheon (1945), p. 410.

20   This moving phrase belongs to F. R. Leavis whom we find at work in the definition of culture between 1930 and 1978 (when he died). See below, ch. 4.

21   Much here is taken from Passmore, *The Perfectibility of Man*, esp. his treatment of the Enlightenment in general and Herder in particular: see pp. 190–238.

22   John Stuart Mill, *The Six Great Humanistic Essays*, ed. A. W. Levi, New York: Washington Square Press (1963), pp. 27–70. Mill's essay on Bentham was written in 1838.

23   Mill, *Six Great Humanistic Essays*, pp. 52ff.

24   J. S. Mill, *Autobiography*, ed. H. Laski; World's Classic Edition, Oxford: Oxford University Press (1952), p. 113.

25   Ibid. p. 125.

26   This point was famously made by W. B. Gallie about 'inherently contested concepts', in his *Philosophy and the Historical Understanding*, New York: Schocken Books (1968).

27   Friedrich Schiller, *On the Aesthetic Education of Man*, Oxford: Oxford University Press (1967), p. 17 (emphasis added).
28   Ibid. p. 34.
29   Max Weber, *The Methodology of the Social Sciences (1903–1917)*, New York: Free Press (1949), pp. 137–63.
30   I follow Terry Eagleton in *The Idea of Culture*, Oxford: Blackwell (2000) but, as many later examples suggest, it is hard to confine the meaning of culture to only three strands.
31   All quotations are from 'Signs of the Times', repr. G. Martin (ed.), *Industrialisation and Culture*, Milton Keynes: Open University Press (1977).
32   Raymond Williams, *The Volunteers*, London: Eyre Methuen (1978), p. 138.
33   Published first in 1890, here cited in Krishan Kumar's edn, *News from Nowhere: or, An Epoch of Rest*; Cambridge Texts in the History of Political Thought, Cambridge University Press (1990).
34   I follow here the judgements of E. P. Thompson in his classic biography, *William Morris: Romantic to Revolutionary*, rev. edn, London: Merlin Press.
35   Letter to *Pall Mall Gazette*, William Morris, *Complete Letters* (*Collected Works*, xix), London: Longmans (1965), p. 315.
36   *William Morris: Political Writings*, ed. A. L. Morton, London: Lawrence and Wishart (1979), p. 121.
37   Ibid. p. 244.
38   Matthew Arnold, *Culture and Anarchy*, ed. J. Dover Wilson, Cambridge: Cambridge University Press (1960), pp. 51–2. My analysis owes everything to Raymond Williams's classic, *Culture and Society, 1780–1950*, London: Chatto and Windus (1958), esp. pp. 71–86, 115–29.
39   L. L. Wittgenstein, *Philosophical Investigations*, Oxford: Basil Blackwell, 1983, para. 71.
40   Arnold, *Culture and Anarchy*, p. 47.
41   Ibid. pp. 53ff.
42   Ibid. p. 66.
43   Ibid. p. 70.
44   Thoughtfully analysed by Stefan Collini in *The English Moralists*, Cambridge: Cambridge University Press (1988).
45   Arnold, *Culture and Anarchy*, pp. 102–4.
46   A point first and most forcefully made by Alisdair MacIntyre, 'A Mistake about Causality in Social Science', in P. Laslett and W. G. Runciman (eds), *Philosophy, Politics and Society*, Oxford: Basil Blackwell (1967), pp. 48–70. The word 'sign' has, however, been regrettably monopolized by semiotics.

47   This phenomenon provides the substantial narratives of Raymond Williams's *Culture and Society*.

48   This sentence, of course, very crudely summarizes the theory of Michel Foucault. For his views concerning the control and voluntary incarceration of whole peoples with the aid of their social sciences, see below, ch. 6.

49   I take the list, if not the argument, from Krishan Kumar, *Utopia and Anti-Utopia*, Oxford: Basil Blackwell (1987).

50   This was Perry Anderson's point in his famous essay, 'Components of the National Culture', repr. in *English Questions*, London: Verso (1994), pp. 92–6.

Chapter 2   Culture and Politics

1   Henry James, *Italian Hours*, Hopewell, NJ: Ecco Press (1987, orig. publ. 1909), pp. 1–63.

2   Ibid. p. 19.

3   Michael Oakeshott, 'The Voice of Poetry in the Conversation of Mankind', *Rationalism in Politics*, rev. edition, Indianapolis: Liberty Fund (1991), pp. 488–541.

4   The classic history of the concept of the state before there was a word for it is Quentin Skinner's *The Foundations of Modern Political Thought*, Cambridge: Cambridge University Press (1978). This brief history of public opinion is taken from Jürgen Habermas, *The Structural Transformation of the Public Sphere*, Cambridge: Polity Press (1989, orig. publ. 1962).

5   Eric Hobsbawm, *The Age of Extremes: The Short Twentieth Century*, London: Michael Joseph (1994).

6   Leon Trotsky, *Literature and Revolution*, Ann Arbor: University of Michigan Press (1960).

7   Ibid. p. 137. Parenthetical phrase inserted from a subsequent point on the same page.

8   Karl Marx and Friedrich Engels, *The German Ideology*, ed. T. J. Arthur, London: Lawrence and Wishart (1970), p. 55.

9   Walter Benjamin, 'The Work of Art in the Age of Mechanical Reproduction', in id. *Illuminations*, London: Jonathan Cape (1970), p. 244.

10   I have been unable to locate this quotation.

11   I take much here from G. A. Cohen, *Marx's Theory of History*, Oxford: Oxford University Press (1975).

12   Antonio Gramsci, *Selections from the Prison Notebooks*, ed. Q. Hoare and G. Nowell Smith, London: Lawrence and Wishart (1971), pp. 26–7.

13 Ibid. p. 419.
14 Ibid. p. 326.
15 Ibid. p. 235.
16 Ibid. pp. 10, 334, 418.
17 Royal Commission, *The Teaching of English in England*, London: Stationery Office (1919).
18 Gramsci, *Prison Notebooks*, pp. 37–43.
19 Ibid. pp. 37–8.
20 I take much of my commentary on the Frankfurt School from Martin Jay's approach in his magnificent and pioneering, *The Dialectical Imagination: A History of the Frankfurt School and the Institute of Social Research, 1923–1950*, London: Heinemann Educational (1973).
21 Quotations are from the Verso (London) edition of 1979. It was first published in German in Amsterdam in 1947.
22 Theodor Adorno, *Prisms*, London: Neville Spearman (1967), p. 87.
23 Theodor Adorno and Max Horkheimer, *The Dialectic of the Enlightenment*, London: Verso (1979), p. 151.
24 Theodor Adorno, *Minima Moralia: Reflections on a Damaged Life*, London: New Left Books (1974), p. 224.

Chapter 3   Culture and the Science of Humanity

1 I am much helped in these definitions by Zygmunt Bauman, *Community*, Cambridge: Polity Press (2001), pp. 9–14.
2 The Kantian hero is affectionately mocked by Iris Murdoch in *The Sovereignty of Good*, London: Routledge and Kegan Paul (1970), pp. 35–41.
3 Bronislaw Malinowski, *A Diary in the Strict Sense of the Term*, New York, Harcourt Books (1967). Written in Polish, this was not translated and published until twenty-five years after his death.
4 James Clifford, *Routes: Travel and Translation in the Late 20th Century*, Cambridge, Mass.: Harvard University Press (1997), p. 154.
5 This is the title of what was to become the classic textbook on the subject by a pupil of Evans-Pritchard: John Beattie, *Other Cultures*, London: Cohen and West (1964).
6 E. Evans-Pritchard, *Social Anthropology*, London: Cohen and West (1951), p. 40.
7 A. R. Radcliffe-Brown, 'On Social Structure', in his *Structure and Function in Primitive Society*, London: Cohen and West (1952), p. 71. The essay first appeared in 1940.

8   The phrase and the idea belong to Michel Foucault in his essay, 'What is an Author?', *Power / Knowledge: Selected Interviews and Other Writings, 1972–1977*, ed. Colin Gordon, New York: Pantheon (1980), p. 96.

9   Sprat, quoted in Basil Willey, *The Seventeenth Background*, Harmondsworth: Penguin (1964), pp. 191–2.

10   I take much in what follows from Clifford Geertz, *Works and Lives: The Anthropologist as Author*, Princeton: Princeton University Press (1988).

11   'The Science of Custom' is the title of ch. 1 of Ruth Benedict's classic *Patterns of Culture*, London: Routledge and Kegan Paul (1935), quoted here from the first paperback edition (1961), pp. 126–7.

12   I cannot arbitrate here as to the justice of Derek Freeman's famous attack on Mead, beyond saying that Freeman also has his anthropological partisanship and that Mead was undoubtedly *there* in both places. See G. Bateson, *Naven: A Survey of the Problems Suggested by a Composite Picture of a New Guinea Tribe*, Stanford: Stanford University Press (1936). For Margaret Mead's *œuvre*, see *Coming of Age: Growing Up in Samoa*, New York: Perennial Classics (2001), and (with Gregory Bateson) *Balinese Character: A Photographic Analysis*, special publication, New York: Academy of Sciences. See also Clifford Geertz, 'Margaret Mead, 1901–1978', in *Biographical Memoirs*, published by the American Academy of Sciences, lviii, Washington DC: National Academy Press (1989).

13   James Morris, *Farewell the Trumpets: An Imperial Retreat*, New York: Harcourt Brace Jovanovich (1978), p. 6.

14   The canonical readings are finely summarized by Richard Bernstein in his *The Restructuring of Social and Political Theory*, Philadelphia: University of Pennsylvania Press (1975). All newcomers to the argument, however, should read W. van O. Quine, 'Two Dogmas of Empiricism', in his *From a Logical Point of View*, Cambridge, Mass.: Harvard University Press (1961), pp. 37–46.

15   See above all, Charles Taylor, *Philosophical Papers*, 2 vols, Cambridge: Cambridge University Press (1985); Alisdair MacIntyre, *After Virtue: A Study in Moral (Theory)*, London: Duckworth (1981).

16   Thomas Kuhn, *The Structure of Scientific Revolutions*, Chicago: Chicago University Press (1962).

17   R. G. Collingwood, *An Autobiography*, Oxford: Clarendon Press (1938), pp. 48–9.

18   Kenneth Burke, *A Grammar of Motives*, New York: Prentice Hall (1945).

19   Ibid. p. 511.
20   Kenneth Burke, *On Symbols and Society*, ed. J. R. Gusfield, Chicago: University of Chicago Press (1989), p. 142.
21   Ibid. pp. 170–1.
22   Clifford Geertz's formula in his *The Interpretation of Cultures*, London: Hutchinson (1975), pp. 444–5.
23   See esp. Michel Foucault, *The Birth of the Clinic*, London: Tavistock Press (1963); *Discipline and Punish*, Harmondsworth: Penguin (1978).
24   In Geertz, *Interpretation of Cultures*, pp. 412–53.
25   Ibid. p. 419.
26   Ibid. p. 443.
27   Ibid. p. 443.
28   Ibid. p. 444.
29   Paraphrased from Quentin Skinner, 'Meaning and Understanding in the History of Ideas', in his *Regarding Method* (*Visions of Politics*, i), Cambridge: Cambridge University Press (2002), pp. 57–89.
30   Bernard Williams, *Moral Luck*, Cambridge: Cambridge University Press (1981), pp. 132–43.
31   Charles Taylor, 'Comparison, History, Truth', in his *Philosophical Arguments*, Cambridge, Mass.: Harvard University Press (1995), p. 150.
32   Ibid. p. 156.

Chapter 4   Culture and Redemption: Literature and Judgement

1   References are to T. S. Eliot, *Collected Poetry and Plays*, London: Faber and Faber (1978).
2   Jessie L. Weston, *From Ritual to Romance*, Cambridge: Cambridge University Press (1980).
3   T. S. Eliot, *Notes towards the Definition of Culture*, New York: Harcourt Brace (1949).
4   Michael Young, *The Rise of the Meritocracy*, Harmondsworth: Penguin (1951).
5   Eliot, *Definition of Culture*, p. 30.
6   Williams, *Culture and Society, 1780–1950*, London: Chatto and Windus (1959), p. 234.
7   I partly paraphrase, partly quote a magnificent essay by F. R. Leavis on purity of thought and feeling in poetry. See F. R. Leavis (ed.), *Selections from 'Scrutiny'*, i, Cambridge: Cambridge University Press, 1968, p. 226.
8   Eliot, *Definition of Culture*, p. 32.

9   Ibid. p. 118.

10   F. R. Leavis and Denys Thompson, *Culture and Environment*, London: Chatto and Windus (1932).

11   George Sturt, *The Wheelwright's Shop*, repr. Cambridge: Cambridge University Press, 1970; George Bourne (Sturt's *nom de plume*), *Portrait of a Village*, London: Duckworth (1922).

12   F. R. Leavis, *D. H. Lawrence: Novelist*, London: Chatto and Windus (1955).

13   The details have been splendidly historicized by Jonathan Rose, in his recent study *The Intellectual Life of the British Working Class*, London and New Haven: Yale University Press (2001).

14   In 1995 I published an admiring biography of Williams, *Raymond Williams: The Life*, London: Routledge, of which this is a summary.

15   Richard Hoggart, *The Uses of Literacy: Aspects of Working Class Life and Entertainment*, Harmondsworth: Penguin (1958).

16   W. Rybczynski, *Home: A Short History of an Idea*, Cambridge: Cambridge University Press (1988), is the sole exception.

17   Hoggart, *Uses of Literacy*, p. 53.

18   Richard Hoggart, *Townscape with Figures: Farnham, Portrait of an English Town*, London: Chatto and Windus (1994).

19   This was published in Britain in three volumes: Richard Hoggart, *A Local Habitation; A Sort of Clowning; An Imagined Life*, Oxford: Oxford University Press (1988, 1991, 1993); and as a single volume in the USA as *A Measured Life: The Times and Places of an Orphaned Intellectual*, New Brunswick, NJ: Transaction Books (1994).

20   As I regret to say the admirable Francis Mulhern does in his *Culture / Metaculture*, London: Routledge (2001).

21   The extra-mural department of Leeds University then included two others whose work is relevant: E. P. Thompson and Alisdair MacIntyre.

22   Raymond Williams, *Border Country*, London: Chatto and Windus (1960).

23   For example in Williams's study of urban-rural literature, *The Country and the City*, London: Chatto and Windus (1973), as well as his excellent novel, *The Fight for Manod*, London: Chatto and Windus (1979).

24   The phrase comes from the title of a deservedly celebrated study of the culture of the powerful: C. Wright Mills, *The Power Elite*, New York: Oxford University Press (1956). See also below, pp. 147–8.

25 Raymond Williams, *Towards 2000*, London: Chatto and Windus (1983), pp. 244–5.

26 In Raymond Williams, *Marxism and Literature*, Oxford: Oxford University Press (1977), chapter 4.

27 Quentin Skinner, 'The Idea of a Cultural Lexicon' (1982), repr. in his *Regarding Method* (*Visions of Politics*, i), Cambridge: Cambridge University Press (2002), pp. 158–74.

28 George Steiner, *Inside Bluebeard's Castle* (The T. S. Eliot Lectures, University of Kent), London: Faber and Faber (1971).

29 Raymond Williams, 'Drama in the Dramatized Society', (inaugural address, Cambridge, 1974), repr. in his *Writing in Society*, London: Verso (1983).

30 A collection of essays was edited by Hall with Martin Jacques after a celebrated conference of the same title, *New Times: The Changing Face of Politics in the 1990s*, London: Lawrence and Wishart (1989).

31 Stuart Hall, 'Cultural Studies: Two Paradigms', *Media, Culture, Society*, 2 (1980), p. 63.

32 Hall and Jacques, *New Times*, p. 128.

Chapter 5   The Social Production of Culture

1 A phrase coined in the book of that name by Frederick Jameson, *The Cultural Turn: Selected Writings on the Post-modern, 1988–1998* London: Verso (1999).

2 'How about English?', as one wag said.

3 This was long a sociological classic, now rather neglected: Talcott Parsons, *The Structure of Social Action*, Glencoe, Ill.: Free Press (1937).

4 The theoretical lead is given by Hall in his extended meditation on class and the formation of identity. See S. Hall (with Paul du Gay), *Questions of Cultural Identity*, London: Sage 1996. For work from the Birmingham Centre following his lead, see in particular Paul Willis, *Learning to Labour: How Working-Class Boys get Working-Class Jobs*, London: Gower (1977), and Stuart Hall and Tony Jefferson (eds), *Resistance Through Rituals*, London: Hutchinson (1976).

5 I owe much here to a conversation with Wolf Lepenies and to his gift of Rolf Lindner's fine book, *The Reportage of Urban Culture: Robert Park and the Chicago School*, Cambridge: Cambridge University Press (1996). See also *The Collected Papers of Robert E. Park*, 3 volumes, Glencoe, Ill.: Free Press (1955); Fred Inglis, *People's Witness: The Journalist in Modern Politics*, London and New Haven: Yale University Press (2002).

6 Lindner, *Reportage of Urban Culture*, p. 41.

7 Ibid. p. 100.

8 Max Weber, 'Politics as a Vocation', in *From Max Weber: Essays in Sociology*, ed. H. H. Gerth and C. Wright Mills, London: Routledge and Kegan Paul (1948), pp. 96ff.

9 Lucien Goldmann, *Le Dieu caché*, Paris: Gallimard (1959); Pierre Bourdieu, *Algeria, 1960: The Disenchantment of the World*, Cambridge: Cambridge University Press (1979); *Outline of a Theory of Practice*, Cambridge: Cambridge University Press (1978); *Distinction: A Social Critique of the Judgement of Taste*, London: Routledge (1984).

10 Émile Durkheim, *On Morality and Society*, ed. Robert Bellah, Chicago: University of Chicago Press (1973).

11 I take much here about the larger history from Perry Anderson, *Lineages of the Absolutist State*, London: New Left Books (1974).

12 Georg Lukacs, *History and Class Consciousness*, London: Merlin Press (1966), first translated into French in 1958 and originally written in 1929.

13 Georg Lukacs, *Goethe and the Spirit of the Age*, London: Merlin Press (1971).

14 Bourdieu, *Algeria*, p. vii, but more fully expounded in Bourdieu, *Outline of a Theory of Practice*.

15 Bourdieu, *Algeria*, p. 5 (emphasis added).

16 Ibid. p. 17.

17 Ibid. p. 22.

18 There are no photographs in Bourdieu. The one I describe comes from Clifford Geertz and Hildred Geertz, *Meaning and Order in Moroccan Society*, New York: Cambridge University Press (1979).

19 Pierre Bourdieu, *Distinction*; see also (with Alain Darbel and Dominique Schnapper) his *The Love of Art: European Art Museums and Their Public*, Cambridge: Polity Press (1991) and *The Rules of Art*, Cambridge: Polity Press (1996).

20 Bourdieu, *Distinction*, p. 139.

21 Ibid. p. 12: 'The Aristocracy of Culture' (pp. 11–17); see also his 'The Production of Belief: Contribution to an Economy of Symbolic Goods', *Media, Culture, and Society*, 2 (1980), pp. 261–95.

22 This was first spotted by Karl Mannheim, in his *Essays on the Sociology of Culture*, London: Routledge and Kegan Paul, (1952).

23 Bourdieu, *Distinction*, p. 142 (original emphasis).

24 See esp. the chapter, 'The Aristocracy of Culture', Bourdieu, *Distinction*.

25 Bourdieu, *Love of Art*; *Rules of Art*, as cited.

26 Bourdieu, *Love of Art*, p. 110.

27 Charles Taylor, *Sources of the Self: The Making of the Modern Identity*, Cambridge: Cambridge University Press (1989), pp. 4, 14, 20, 42 and *passim*.

28 See Clifford Geertz, *The Social History of an Indonesian Town*, Cambridge: MIT Press (1965).

29 Repr. first in R. S. Peters (ed.), *Plowden and After*, London: Routledge (1969), and then in Basil Bernstein, *Class, Codes, Control*, i, pp. 190–201. London: Routledge and Kegan Paul (1971).

30 Basil Bernstein, 'On the Classification and Framing of Educational Knowledge', in *Class, Codes, Control*, i, pp. 202–29.

31 Basil Bernstein, 'The Structuring of Pedagogical Discourse', in *Class, Codes, Control*, iv, London: Routledge (1989).

32 Basil Bernstein, *Pedagogy, Symbolic Control, Identity*, rev. edn, London: Taylor and Francis (2000).

33 I have in mind the use made of Hume in Avishai Margalit, *The Decent Society*, Cambridge, Mass: Harvard University Press (1996).

34 Richard Rorty, *Philosophy and the Mirror of Nature*, Oxford: Basil Blackwell (1980); *Contingency, Irony and Solidarity*, Cambridge: Cambridge University Press (1989).

35 Raymond Williams, *The Long Revolution*, London: Chatto and Windus (1961), p. 48.

36 Raymond Williams, *Marxism and Literature*, Oxford University Press (1977), pp. 133–4.

37 I implicitly refer to the title of a work by a distinguished perfectionist of our day: Jürgen Habermas, *Knowledge and Human Interests*, London: Heinemann Educational (1974).

38 Charles Taylor, 'Self-Interpreting Animals', in his *Human Agency and Language* (*Philosophical Papers*, ii), Cambridge: Cambridge University Press (1985), pp. 45–76.

Chapter 6   Culture and Postmodernism: The Good, the True and the Beautiful

1 Antonio Gramsci, *Selections from the Prison Notebooks*, ed. Q. Hoare and G. Nowell Smith, London: Lawrence and Wishart (1971), p. 228.

2 Each story has been plainly and vividly told by Timothy Garton Ash (who was there in Prague). See his trilogy, *The Uses of*

Adversity; *The Magic Lantern*; *The Polish Revolution*, Cambridge: Granta (1989–91).

3   The most vehement theorist of politics as ordered enmity is the quasi-Nazi Carl Schmitt, for whom politics was defined by a nation's discovery and maintenance of its enemies. See his *The Concept of the Political*, New Brunswick, NJ: Rutgers University Press (1976).

4   Perry Anderson, *The Origins of Postmodernity*, London: Verso (1998).

5   Jean-François Lyotard, *La Condition postmoderne*, Paris: Gallimard (1979).

6   The 'knowledge society' is now something of a cliché. The first such usage was probably by Mark Poster, *The Mode of Information: Poststructuralism and Social Context*, Chicago: University of Chicago Press (1990); the most comprehensive and ambitious by Manuel Castells, in his now-celebrated *The Information Society*, Oxford: Blackwell, 3 vols (1996–9).

7   I suggest this as the defining feature of contemporary systems of knowledge and therefore of culture in *The Management of Ignorance*, Oxford: Blackwell (1985).

8   David Harvey, *The Condition of Postmodernity*, Oxford: Blackwell (1990). His argument was helped by Stuart Hall and Martin Jacques (eds), *The Politics of Thatcherism*, London: Lawrence and Wishart (1984), esp. Robin Murray, 'The Benetton Economy', pp. 117–22.

9   See also Richard Sennett, *The Corrosion of Character: The Personal Consequences of Working in the New Capitalism*, New York: Norton (1998).

10   This was clearly argued by Anthony Smith in his *Software for the Self: Culture and Technology*, London: Faber (1996).

11   See esp. Paul Hirst and Graham Thompson, *Globalization in Question*, Cambridge: Polity Press (1996), and David Held, *Democracy and the Global Order: From the Modern State to Cosmopolitan Government*, Stanford: Stanford University Press (1995).

12   I borrow ideas here from Erik Erikson's classic *Identity: Youth and the Social Crisis*, New York: W. W. Norton (1968), and more particularly from an unpublished paper by Charles Taylor, 'Modernity and Identity' (1997), to whom I am most grateful.

13   Alphonse de Lamartine, 'Déclaration de principes', *Œuvres complètes*, Paris (1869), iii, p. 179; James A. Froude, *Thomas Carlyle: A History of His Life in London, 1834–1881*, 2 vols, London (1884), pp. 290–1.

14 Most usefully and good-temperedly John Tomlinson, in his *Globalization and Culture*, Cambridge: Polity Press (1999). For a much more polemical account, see John Gray, *False Dawn: The Delusions of Global Capitalism*, London: Granta (1998).

15 The nearest thing to an anthropology of the rich which we have is now somewhat dated: C. Wright Mills, *The Power Elite*, New York: Free Press (1970).

16 Joseph Stiglitz, *Globalization and Its Discontents*, New York: Norton (2003).

17 Ibid. p. 197.

18 I borrow phrases here once more from Clifford Geertz's *The Interpretation of Cultures* (1975), p. 220.

19 This was told by the distinguished anthropologist Paul Rabinow, in his *French DNA: Trouble in Purgatory*, Chicago: University of Chicago Press (1999).

20 Edward Said, *Culture and Imperialism*, New York: Random House (1993).

21 Seyla Benhabib, *The Claims of Culture: Equality and Diversity in the Global Era*, Princeton: Princeton University Press (2002).

22 Ibid. p. 21.

23 Homi Bhabha, *The Location of Culture*, London: Routledge (1994), p. 70.

24 Fredric Jameson, *The Cultural Turn: Selected Writings on the Postmodern, 1988–1998*, London: Verso (1999), p. 25.

25 To pick a quartet of names at random since 1980: John Ashbery's and James Merrill's poems, Don DeLillo's and Martin Amis's novels.

26 Richard Rorty, *Philosophy and the Mirror of Nature*, Oxford: Basil Blackwell (1980).

27 Ibid. pp. 122–3.

28 This oxymoron is the title of a paper by Bernard Williams in his *Moral Luck: Philosophical Papers, 1973–1980*, Cambridge: Cambridge University Press (1981), pp. 132–43.

29 I take much in what follows also from Bernard Williams, *Ethics and the Limits of Philosophy*, Cambridge, Mass.: Harvard University Press (1985), ch. 9.

30 Readers may care to look up Judith Butler's *Excitable Speech: A Politics of the Performative*, London: Routledge (1997), and her *Gender Trouble: Feminism and the Subversion of Identity*, London: Routledge (1999); Gayatri Spivak, *A Critique of Postcolonial Reason: Towards a History of the Vanishing Present*, Cambridge, Mass.: Harvard University Press (1999).

31 Kate Millett, *Sexual Politics*, New York: Pantheon (1970); Germaine Greer, *The Female Eunuch*, London: Picador (1970);

Andrea Dworkin, *Pornography: Men Possessing Women*, London: Women's Press (1981).

32   Luce Irigaray, *The Irigaray Reader*, M. Whitford (ed), Oxford: Blackwell (1991); Nancy Chodorow, *The Reproduction of Mothering*, Berkeley: University of California Press (1978); Jessica Benjamin, *The Bonds of Love*, London: Virago (1990).

33   It is baffling, as Philip Fisher points out, that Descartes omits fear. See Fisher's *The Vehement Passions*, Princeton: Princeton University Press (2002).

34   In this I follow a lead given by Miranda Fricker and Jennifer Hornby (eds), *Feminism in Philosophy*, Cambridge: Cambridge University Press (2000), esp. the contribution by Susan James, 'Feminism in the Philosophy of Mind', pp. 29–48.

35   The relevant works are Annette Baier, *Moral Prejudice: Essays on Ethics*, Cambridge, Mass.: Harvard University Press (1994); Onora O'Neill, *A Question of Trust*, London: BBC/Penguin (2002). In this connection, see also Emma Rothschild's valuable book, *Economic Sentiments: Adam Smith, Condorcet, and the Enlightenment*, Cambridge, Mass.: Harvard University Press (2001).

36   Martha Nussbaum, esp. *Upheavals of Thought: The Intelligence of Emotions*, Cambridge: Cambridge University Press (2001); *Love's Knowledge*, Oxford: Oxford University Press (1990).

37   This is Thomas Nagel's instance, in his essay 'What Is It Like to Be a Bat?', in his *Mortal Questions*, Cambridge: Cambridge University Press (1979).

38   Christopher Lasch, *The Culture of Narcissism*, New York: Basic Books (1980).

39   Robert Hughes, *Culture of Complaint*, Oxford: Oxford University Press (1993).

40   Richard Rorty, *Truth and Progress* (*Philosophical Papers*, iii), Cambridge: Cambridge University Press (1998), pp. 228–46.

41   Wolf Lepenies, *Exile and Emigration: The Survival of 'German Culture'*, Princeton: Institute for Advanced Study, School of Social Science, Occasional Paper 7, March (2000).

42   Ibid. pp. 2–3.

43   A definition of culture's synonym 'ethos' taught to me by Adam Morton years ago in Bristol, to whom I am most grateful.

44   Stanley Cavell, *Conditions Handsome and Unhandsome: The Constitution of Emersonian Perfectionism*, Chicago: University of Chicago Press (1990), pp. 50–6.

45   Ibid. p. 55.

46   Ibid. p. 57.

47 Jürgen Habermas, 'Modernity: An Incomplete Project', Adorno lecture (1980), *New German Critique*, Winter (1981), pp. 3–15.

48 Guy Debord, *The Society of the Spectacle*, Detroit: Red and Black Books (1984).

49 This is Richard Howells's point in his impressive *Visual Culture*, Cambridge: Polity Press (2003).

50 *Social Trends*, London: Stationery Office (2001).

51 I offer an account of this variety in my *Media Theory*, Oxford: Blackwell (1990), 'The Problem of Audience', pp. 134–55.

52 Elaine Scarry, *On Beauty and Being Just*, London: Duckworth (2000), pp. 29, 31.

Bibliography

Adorno, T. (1967) *Prisms*. London: Neville Spearman.

Adorno, T. (1974) *Minima Moralia: Reflections on a Damaged Life*. London: New Left Books.

Adorno, T. (1997) *Aesthetic Theory*. London: Athlone Press.

Adorno, T., and Horkheimer, M. (1979) *Dialectic of Enlightenment*. London: Verso (orig. publ. 1944).

Anderson, P. (1974) *Lineages of the Absolutist State*. London: New Left Books.

Anderson, P. (1994) 'Components of the National Culture', in P. Anderson, *English Questions*. London: Verso, pp. 48–104.

Anderson, P. (1998) *The Origins of Postmodernity*. London: Verso.

Arnold, M. (1960) *Culture and Anarchy*, ed. J. Dover Wilson. Cambridge: Cambridge University Press.

Austin, J. L. (1961) *Philosophical Papers*, ed. J. O. Urmson and G. J. Warnock. Oxford: Clarendon Press.

Baier, A. (1994) *Moral Prejudice: Essays on Ethics*. Cambridge, Mass.: Harvard University Press.

Bateson, G. (1936) *Naven: A Survey of the Problems Suggested by a Composite Picture of a New Guinea Tribe*. Stanford: Stanford University Press.

Bauman, Z. (2001) *Community*. Cambridge: Polity Press.

Beattie, J. (1964) *Other Cultures*. London: Cohen and West.

Benedict, R. (1935) *Patterns of Culture*. London: Routledge and Kegan Paul.

Benhabib, S. (2002) *The Claims of Culture: Equality and Diversity in the Global Era*. Princeton: Princeton University Press.

Benjamin, J. (1990) *The Bonds of Love*. London: Virago.

Benjamin, W. (1970) *Illuminations*. London: Jonathan Cape.

Berger, P., and Luckmann, T. (1967) *The Social Construction of Reality*. Harmondsworth: Allen Lane, Penguin Press.

Berlin, I. (1976) *Vico and Herder: Two Studies in the History of Ideas*. London: Hogarth Press.

Bernstein, B. (1971) *Class, Codes, Control*, i. London: Routledge and Kegan Paul.

Bernstein, B. (1989) *Class, Codes, Control*, iv. London: Routledge.

Bernstein, B. (2000) *Pedagogy, Symbolic Control, Identity*, revd edn. London: Taylor and Francis.

Bernstein, R. (1975) *The Restructuring of Social and Political Theory*. Philadelphia: University of Pennsylvania Press.

Bhabha, H. (1994) *The Location of Culture*. London: Routledge.

Bourdieu, P. (1978) *Outline of a Theory of Practice*. Cambridge: Cambridge University Press.

Bourdieu, P. (1979) *Algeria, 1960: The Disenchantment of the World*. Cambridge: Cambridge University Press.

Bourdieu, P. (1980) 'The Production of Belief: Contribution to an Economy of Symbolic Goods', *Media, Culture and Society*, 2, pp. 261–95.

Bourdieu, P. (1984) *Distinction: A Social Critique of the Judgement of Taste*. London: Routledge.

Bourdieu, P. (with A. Darbel and D. Schnapper) (1991) *The Love of Art: European Art Museums and Their Public*. Cambridge: Polity Press.

Bourdieu, P. (1996) *The Rules of Art: Genesis and Structure of the Literary Field*. Cambridge: Polity Press.

Bourne, G. (1922) *Portrait of a Village*. London: Duckworth.

Burke, K. (1945) *A Grammar of Motives*. New York: Prentice Hall.

Burke, K. (1989) *On Symbols and Society*, ed. J. R. Gusfield. Chicago: University of Chicago Press.

Burrow, J., Collini, S., and Winch, D. (1983) *That Noble Science of Politics*. Cambridge: Cambridge University Press.

Butler, J. (1997) *Excitable Speech: A Politics of the Performative*. London: Routledge.

Butler, J. (1999) *Gender Trouble: Feminism and the Subversion of Identity*. London: Routledge.

Castells, M. (1996–9) *The Information Society*, 3 vols. Oxford: Blackwell.

Chodorow, N. (1978) *The Reproduction of Mothering*. Berkeley: University of California Press.

Clifford, J. (1997) *Routes: Travel and Translation in the Late 20th Century*. Cambridge, Mass.: Harvard University Press.

Cohen, G. A. (1975) *Marx's Theory of History*. Oxford: Oxford University Press.

Collingwood, R. G. (1938) *An Autobiography.* Oxford: Clarendon Press.

Collini, S. (1988) *The English Moralists.* Cambridge: Cambridge University Press.

Debord, G. (1984) *The Society of the Spectacle.* Detroit: Red and Black Books.

Durkheim, E. *On Morality and Society,* ed. R. Bellah. Chicago: University of Chicago Press.

Dworkin, A. (1981) *Pornography: Men Possessing Women.* London: Women's Press.

Eagleton, T. (2000) *The Idea of Culture.* Oxford: Blackwell.

Eliot, T. S. (1949) *Notes towards the Definition of Culture.* New York: Harcourt Brace.

Eliot, T. S. (1978) *Collected Poetry and Plays.* London: Faber and Faber.

Erikson, E. (1972) *Identity: Youth and the Social Crisis.* New York: W. W. Norton.

Evans-Pritchard, E. (1951) *Social Anthropology.* London: Cohen and West.

Fisher, P. (2002) *The Vehement Passions.* Princeton: Princeton University Press.

Foucault, M. (1963) *The Birth of the Clinic.* London: Tavistock Press.

Foucault, M. (1978) *Discipline and Punish.* Harmondsworth: Penguin.

Foucault, M. (1980) *Power/Knowledge: Selected Interviews and Other Writings, 1972–1977* (ed. C. Gordon). New York: Pantheon.

Fricker, M., and Hornby, J. (eds), *Feminism in Philosophy.* Cambridge: Cambridge University Press.

Froude, J. A. (1884) *Thomas Carlyle: A History of His Life in London, 1834–1881,* 2 vols. London.

Gallie, W. B. (1968) *Philosophy and the Historical Understanding.* New York: Schocken Books.

Garton Ash, T. (1989) *The Uses of Adversity.* Cambridge: Granta.

Garton Ash, T. (1990) *The Magic Lantern.* Cambridge: Granta.

Garton Ash, T. (1991) *The Polish Revolution.* Cambridge: Granta.

Geertz, C. (1965) *The Social History of an Indonesian Town.* Cambridge: MIT Press.

Geertz, C. (1975) *The Interpretation of Cultures.* London: Hutchinson.

Geertz, C. (1988) *Works and Lives: The Anthropologist as Author.* Princeton: Princeton University Press.

Geertz, C. (1989) 'Margaret Mead, 1901–1978', in National Academy of Science, *Biographical Memoirs.* Washington, DC: National Academy Press.

Geertz, C., and Geertz, H. (1975) *Kinship in Bali*. Chicago: University of Chicago Press.

Geertz, C., and Geertz, H. (1979) *Meaning and Order in Moroccan Society*. New York: Cambridge University Press.

Goldmann, L. (1959) *Le Dieu caché*. Paris: Gallimard.

Gramsci, A. (1971) *Selections from the Prison Notebooks*, ed. Q. Hoare and G. Nowell Smith. London: Lawrence and Wishart.

Gray, J. (1998) *False Dawn: The Delusions of Global Capitalism*. London: Granta.

Greer, G. (1970) *The Female Eunuch*. London: Picador.

Habermas, J. (1981) 'Modernity: An Incomplete Project', Adorno lecture. *New German Critique*, winter.

Habermas, J. (1989) *The Structural Transformation of the Public Sphere*. Cambridge: Polity Press (orig. publ. 1962).

Hall, S. (1980) 'Cultural Studies: Two Paradigms', *Media, Culture, Society*, 2, pp. 57–72.

Hall, S. (with P. du Gay) (1996) *Questions of Cultural Identity*. London: Sage.

Hall, S., and Jacques, M. (eds) (1984) *The Politics of Thatcherism*. London: Lawrence and Wishart.

Hall, S., and Jacques, M. (1989) *New Times: the Changing Face of Politics in the 1990s*. London: Lawrence and Wishart.

Harvey, D. (1990) *The Condition of Postmodernity*. Oxford: Blackwell.

Held, D. (1995) *Democracy and the Global Order: From the Modern State to Cosmopolitan Governance*. Stanford: Stanford University Press.

Herder, J. G. (1969) *J. G. Herder on Social and Political Culture*, ed. F. M. Barnard. Cambridge: Cambridge University Press.

Hirst, P., and Thompson, G. (1996) *Globalization in Question*. Cambridge: Polity Press.

Hobsbawm, E. (1994) *The Age of Extremes: The Short Twentieth Century*. London: Michael Joseph.

Hoggart, R. (1958) *The Uses of Literacy: Aspects of Working Class Life and Entertainment*, Harmondsworth: Penguin.

Hoggart, R. (1988) *A Local Habitation*. London: Chatto and Windus.

Hoggart, R. (1991) *A Sort of Clowning*. Oxford: Oxford University Press.

Hoggart, R. (1993) *An Imagined Life*. Oxford: Oxford University Press.

Hoggart, R. (1994) *A Measured Life: The Times and Places of an Orphaned Intellectual*. New Brunswick, NJ: Transaction Books.

Hoggart, R. (1994) *Townscape with Figures: Farnham, Portrait of an English Town*. London: Chatto and Windus.

Howells, R. (2003) *Visual Culture*. Cambridge: Polity Press.

Hughes, R. (1993) *Culture of Complaint*. Oxford: Oxford University Press.

Inglis, F. (1985) *The Management of Ignorance*. Oxford: Blackwell.

Inglis, F. (1995) *Raymond Williams: The Life*. London: Routledge.

Inglis, F. (2002) *People's Witness: The Journalist in Modern Politics*. London and New Haven: Yale University Press.

James, H. (1987) *Italian Hours*. Hopewell, NJ: Ecco Press (orig. publ. 1909).

Jameson, F. (1999) *The Cultural Turn: Selected Writings on the Postmodern, 1988–1998*. London: Verso.

Jay, M. (1973) *The Dialectical Imagination: A History of the Frankfurt School and the Institute of Social Research, 1923–1950*. London: Heinemann Educational.

Irigaray, L. (1991) *The Irigaray Reader*, ed. M. Whitford. Oxford: Blackwell.

Kant, I. (1954) *The Critique of Pure Reason*, trans. L. W. Beck. Indianapolis: Bobbs-Merrill.

Kuhn, T. (1962) *The Structure of Scientific Revolutions*. Chicago: Chicago University Press.

Kumar, K. (1987) *Utopia and Anti-Utopia*. Oxford: Basil Blackwell.

Lamartine, A. de (1869) *Œuvres complètes*. Paris.

Lasch, C. (1980) *The Culture of Narcissism*. New York: Basic Books.

Leavis, F. R. (1955) *D. H. Lawrence: Novelist*. London: Chatto and Windus.

Leavis, F. R. (ed.) (1968) *Selections from 'Scrutiny'*, i. Cambridge: Cambridge University Press.

Leavis, F. R., and Thompson, D. (1932) *Culture and Environment*. London: Chatto and Windus.

Lepenies, W. (2000) *Exile and Emigration: The Survival of 'German Culture'*. Princeton: Institute for Advanced Study, School of Social Science, Occasional Paper 7, March.

Lewis, O. (1963) *The Culture of Poverty*. New York: Holt Rhinehart.

Lindner, W. (1996) *The Reporting of Urban Culture: Robert Park and the Chicago School*. Cambridge: Cambridge University Press.

Lukacs, G. (1966) *History and Class Consciousness*. London: Merlin Press.

Lukacs, G. (1971) *Goethe and the Spirit of the Age*. London: Merlin Press.

MacIntyre, A. (1967) 'A Mistake about Causality in Social Science', in P. Laslett and W. G. Runciman (eds), *Philosophy, Politics and Society*, pp. 48–70. Oxford: Basil Blackwell.

MacIntyre, A. (1981) *After Virtue: A Study in Moral Theory*. London: Duckworth, 1981.

Malinowski, B. (1967) *A Diary in the Strict Sense of the Term.* New York: Harcourt Books.

Mannheim, K. (1952) *Essays on the Sociology of Culture.* London: Routledge and Kegan Paul.

Margalit, A. (1996) *The Decent Society.* Cambridge Mass: Harvard University Press.

Martin, G. (1977) *Industrialization and Culture.* Milton Keynes: Open University Press.

Marx, K., and Engels, F. (1970) *The German Ideology,* ed. T. J. Arthur. London: Lawrence and Wishart.

Matisse, H. (1945) in R. Goldwater and M. Treves (eds), *Artists on Art,* New York: Pantheon.

Mead, M. (2001) *Coming of Age: Growing Up in Samoa.* New York: Perennial Classics.

Mead, M., and Bateson, G. (1942) *Balinese Character: A Photographic Analysis,* special publication. New York: Academy of Sciences.

Mill, J. S. (1952) *Autobiography,* ed. H. Laski. (World's Classic edition) Oxford: Oxford University Press.

Mill, J. S. (1963) *The Six Great Humanistic Essays,* ed. A. W. Levi. New York: Washington Square Press.

Millett, K. (1970) *Sexual Politics.* New York: Pantheon.

Morris, J. (1978) *Farewell the Trumpets: An Imperial Retreat.* New York: Harcourt Brace Jovanovich.

Morris, W. (1965) *Complete Letters* (*Collected Works,* xix). London: Longmans, 1965.

Morris, W. (1979) *William Morris: Political Writings.* ed. A. L. Morton. London: Lawrence and Wishart.

Morris, W. (1990) *News from Nowhere: or, An Epoch of Rest,* ed. K. Kumar; Cambridge Texts in the History of Political Thought. Cambridge: Cambridge University Press.

Mulhern, F. (2001) *Culture / Metaculture.* London: Routledge.

Murdoch, I. (1970) *The Sovereignty of Good.* London: Routledge and Kegan Paul.

Nagel, T. (1979) *Mortal Questions.* Cambridge: Cambridge University Press.

Nussbaum, M. (1990) *Love's Knowledge.* Oxford: Oxford University Press.

Nussbaum, M. (2001) *Upheavals of Thought: The Intelligence of Emotions.* Cambridge: Cambridge University Press.

Oakeshott, M. (1991) *Rationalism in Politics*; rev. edn. Indianapolis: Liberty Fund.

Offe, C. (1990) *Disorganised Capitalism.* Cambridge: Polity Press.

O'Neill, O. (2002) *A Question of Trust.* London: BBC/Penguin.

Park, R. E. (1955) *Collected Papers,* 3 vols. Glencoe, Ill.: Free Press.

Passmore, J. (1970) *The Perfectibility of Man*. London: Duckworth.

Popper, K. (1953) *The Logic of Scientific Discovery*. London: Routledge and Kegan Paul.

Popper, K. (1966) *Conjectures and Refutations*. London: Routledge and Kegan Paul.

Poster, M. (1990) *The Mode of Information: Poststructuralism and Social Context*. Chicago: University of Chicago Press.

Rabinow, P. (1999) *French DNA: Trouble in Purgatory*. Chicago: University of Chicago Press.

Radcliffe-Brown, A. R. (1952) *Structure and Function in Primitive Society*. London: Cohen and West.

Rorty, R. (1980) *Philosophy and the Mirror of Nature*. Oxford: Basil Blackwell.

Rorty, R. (1989) *Contingency, Irony and Solidarity*. Cambridge: Cambridge University Press.

Rorty, R. (1998) *Truth and Progress* (*Philosophical Papers*, iii). Cambridge: Cambridge University Press.

Rose, J. (2001) *The Intellectual Life of the British Working Class*. London and New Haven: Yale University Press.

Rothschild, E. (2001) *Economic Sentiments: Adam Smith, Condorcet, and the Enlightenment*. Cambridge, Mass.: Harvard University Press.

Royal Commission (1919) *The Teaching of English in England*. London: Stationery Office.

Rybczynski, W. (1988) *Home: A Short History of an Idea*. Cambridge: Cambridge University Press.

Said, E. (1985) *Orientalism*. Harmondsworth: Penguin.

Said, R. (1993) *Culture and Imperialism*. New York: Random House.

Scarry, E. (2000) *On Beauty and Being Just*. London: Duckworth.

Schiller, F. (1967) *On the Aesthetic Education of Man*. Oxford: Oxford University Press.

Searle, J. (1995) *The Construction of Social Reality*. London: Allen Lane.

Sennett, R. (1998) *The Corrosion of Character: The Personal Consequences of Working in the New Capitalism*. New York: Norton.

Skinner, Q. (1978) *The Foundations of Modern Political Thought*. Cambridge: Cambridge University Press.

Skinner, Q. (1988) *Meaning and Context*, ed. J. Tully. Princeton: Princeton University Press.

Skinner, Q. (2002) *Regarding Method* (*Visions of Politics*, i). Cambridge: Cambridge University Press.

Smith, A. (1996) *Software for the Self: Culture and Technology*. London: Faber.

Spivak, G. (1999) *A Critique of Postcolonial Reason: toward a history of the vanishing present.* Cambridge, Mass.: Harvard University Press.

Steiner, G. (1971) *Inside Bluebeard's Castle.* London: Faber and Faber.

Sturt, G. (1970) *The Wheelwright's Shop.* Cambridge: Cambridge University Press.

Taylor, C. (1975) *Hegel.* Cambridge: Cambridge University Press.

Taylor, C. (1985) *Human Agency and Language (Philosophical Papers,* ii). Cambridge: Cambridge University Press.

Taylor, C. (1989) *Sources of the Self: The Making of the Modern Identity.* Cambridge: Cambridge University Press.

Taylor, C. (1995) *Philosophical Arguments.* Cambridge, Mass.: Harvard University Press.

Thompson, E. P. (1977) *William Morris: Romantic to Revolutionary,* rev. edn. London: Merlin Press.

Tomlinson, J. (1999) *Globalization and Culture.* Cambridge: Polity Press.

Trotsky, L. (1960) *Literature and Revolution.* Ann Arbor: University of Michigan Press.

Weber, M. (1947) *The Theory of Social and Economic Organisation,* ed. T. Parsons. New York: Free Press.

Weber, M. (1948) *From Max Weber: Essays in Sociology,* ed. H. H. Gerth and C. Wright Mills. London: Routledge and Kegan Paul.

Weber, M. (1949) *The Methodology of the Social Sciences (1903–1917).* New York: Free Press.

Weston, J. L. (1980) *From Ritual to Romance.* Cambridge: Cambridge University Press.

Willey, B. (2002) *The Seventeenth Century Background.* Harmondsworth: Penguin.

Williams, B. (1981) *Moral Luck.* Cambridge: Cambridge University Press.

Williams, B. (1985) *Ethics and the Limits of Philosophy.* Cambridge, Mass.: Harvard University Press.

Williams, R. (1958) *Culture and Society, 1780–1950.* London: Chatto and Windus.

Williams, R. (1960) *Border Country.* London: Chatto and Windus.

Williams, R. (1961) *The Long Revolution.* London: Chatto and Windus.

Williams, R. (1973) *The Country and the City.* London: Chatto and Windus.

Williams, R. (1977) *Marxism and Literature.* Oxford: Oxford University Press.

Williams, R. (1978) *The Volunteers.* London: Eyre Methuen.

Williams, R. (1979) *The Fight for Manod*. London: Chatto and Windus.

Williams, R. (1980) *Writing in Society*. London: Verso.

Williams, R. (1983) *Towards 2000*. London: Chatto and Windus.

Willis, P. (1977) *Learning to Labour*. Farnborough: Saxon House.

Wittgenstein, L. L. (1983) *Philosophical Investigations*. Oxford: Basil Blackwell.

Wright Mills, C. (1956) *The Power Elite*. New York: Free Press.

Young, M. (1951) *The Rise of the Meritocracy*. Harmondsworth: Penguin.

Index